PRAISE FOR
Lives of American Women

"Finally! The majority of students—by which I mean women—will have the opportunity to read biographies of women from our nation's past. (Men can read them too, of course!) The Lives of American Women series features an eclectic collection of books, readily accessible to students who will be able to see the contributions of women in many fields over the course of our history. Long overdue, these books will be a valuable resource for teachers, students, and the public at large."
—COKIE ROBERTS,
author of *Founding Mothers* and *Ladies of Liberty*

"Just what any professor wants: books that will intrigue, inform, and fascinate students! These short, readable biographies of American women—specifically designed for classroom use—give instructors an appealing new option to assign to their history students."
—MARY BETH NORTON,
Mary Donlon Alger Professor of American History,
Cornell University

"For educators keen to include women in the American story, but hampered by the lack of thoughtful, concise scholarship, here comes Lives of American Women, embracing Abigail Adams's counsel to John—'remember the ladies.' And high time, too!"
—LESLEY S. HERRMANN,
Executive Director, The Gilder Lehrman
Institute of American History

"Students both in the general survey course and in specialized offerings like my course on U.S. women's history can get a great understanding of an era from a short biography. Learning a lot about a single but complex character really helps to deepen appreciation of what women's lives were like in the past."
—PATRICIA CLINE COHEN,
University of California, Santa Barbara

"Biographies are, indeed, back. Not only will students read them, biographies provide an easy way to demonstrate particularly important historical themes or ideas. . . . Undergraduate readers will be challenged to think more deeply about what it means to be a woman, citizen, and political actor. . . . I am eager to use this in my undergraduate survey and specialty course."

—JENNIFER THIGPEN,
Washington State University, Pullman

"These books are, above all, fascinating stories that will engage and inspire readers. They offer a glimpse into the lives of key women in history who either defied tradition or who successfully maneuvered in a man's world to make an impact. The stories of these vital contributors to American history deliver just the right formula for instructors looking to provide a more complicated and nuanced view of history."

—ROSANNE LICHATIN,
2005 Gilder Lehrman Preserve American History
Teacher of the Year

"The Lives of American Women authors raise all of the big issues I want my classes to confront—and deftly fold their arguments into riveting narratives that maintain students' excitement."

—WOODY HOLTON,
author of *Abigail Adams*

Lives of American Women

Carol Berkin, Series Editor

Westview Press is pleased to launch Lives of American Women. Selected and edited by renowned women's historian Carol Berkin, these brief, affordably priced biographies are designed for use in undergraduate courses. Rather than taking a comprehensive approach, each biography focuses instead on a particular aspect of a woman's life that is emblematic of her time or made her a pivotal figure in her era. The emphasis is on a "good read," featuring accessible writing and compelling narratives, without sacrificing sound scholarship and academic integrity. Primary sources at the end of each biography reveal the subject's perspective in her own words. Study questions and an annotated bibliography support the student reader.

Shirley Chisholm

Catalyst for Change, 1926–2005

LIVES OF AMERICAN WOMEN

Carol Berkin, Series Editor

WESTVIEW
PRESS

A Member of the Perseus Books Group

This book is dedicated to the students of Brooklyn College of the City University of New York—our future "catalysts for change."

Westview Press was founded in 1975 in Boulder, Colorado, by notable publisher and intellectual Fred Praeger. Westview Press continues to publish scholarly titles and high-quality undergraduate- and graduate-level textbooks in core social science disciplines. With books developed, written, and edited with the needs of serious nonfiction readers, professors, and students in mind, Westview Press honors its long history of publishing books that matter.

Find us on the World Wide Web at www.westviewpress.com.
Every effort has been made to secure required permissions for all text, images, maps, and other art reprinted in this volume.

Westview Press books are available at special discounts for bulk purchases in the United States by corporations, institutions, and other organizations. For more information, please contact the Special Markets Department at the Perseus Books Group, 2300 Chestnut Street, Suite 200, Philadelphia, PA 19103, or call (800) 810-4145, ext. 5000, or e-mail special.markets@perseusbooks.com.

Designed by Brent Wilcox

Library of Congress Cataloging-in-Publication Data

Winslow, Barbara, 1945–
    Shirley Chisholm : catalyst for change / Barbara Winslow.
        pages cm. — (Lives of American women)
    Includes bibliographical references and index.
    ISBN 978-0-8133-4769-1 (pbk.) — ISBN 978-0-8133-4770-7 (e-book) 1. Chisholm, Shirley, 1924–2005. 2. African American legislators—Biography. 3. Women legislators—United States—Biography. 4. Legislators—United States—Biography. 5. United States. Congress. House—Biography. 6. Teachers—United States—Biography. 7. Presidential candidates—United States—Biography. 8. United States—Race relations. I. Title.
    E840.8.C48W56 2014
    328.73'092—dc23
    [B]
                                    2013026485

10 9 8 7 6 5 4 3 2 1

CONTENTS

SERIES EDITOR'S FOREWORD

She came out of a modest neighborhood in Brooklyn, by way of a childhood in Barbados. She had grown up without the advantages of an Ivy League education, family wealth—or white skin. Yet Shirley Chisholm made her mark on American politics: as the first African American and the first African American woman to mount a serious campaign for the US presidency. In this dynamic biography, Barbara Winslow, who established the Shirley Chisholm Project of Brooklyn Women's Activism, reconstructs the life of this independent woman who proudly proclaimed herself "unbought and unbossed" and came to be known as "fighting Shirley Chisholm."

Chisholm was a small woman, but she had big ambitions and strong views on what America's priorities ought to be in the twentieth century. She challenged the closed circle of party bosses in New York's Democratic Party, and she demanded that government on every level pay attention to the needs of immigrants and the poor, whether black, brown, or white, who needed better housing, access to education, and decent wages. She was also an outspoken champion of racial and gender equality. Chisholm's success in politics rested in part on her drive and determination, but it also rested on a seeming paradox: she was often a rebel, refusing to accept business as usual in the smoke-filled rooms of her local Democratic Party clubs or in the halls of Congress, yet she just as often was a realist, forming alliances with establishment politicians and compromising on issues in order to enhance her political influence. She was thus a grassroots organizer, but she was also a player on the grand stage of Washington politics. She was, in fact, a consummate politician who might have gone all the way to the White House if she did not have to face what were then the overwhelming obstacles of class, race, and gender. She always saw herself first and foremost as a teacher and organizer. When Chisholm announced she was a candidate for president, the response ran the gamut from amusement to derision to anger to support. There were those who viewed her campaign as a joke, those who viewed it as a distraction from the serious struggle for the presidency, those who opposed her campaign solely because of her gender, and those who admired her but knew that her lack of funds and inadequate campaign organization doomed her candidacy from the start. Chisholm herself recognized that she would not succeed, but she never viewed her candidacy as simply symbolic, or as a mere gesture. She wanted to use her candidacy to bring critical issues to the attention of the American people, chief among them racial and gender equality. Her public role coincided with the rise of the civil rights and feminist movements, and her career intertwined with both of them. Yet she always said that being black was less of a liability than being female—a judgment that suggests how difficult the path to gender equality was and remains today.

In examining and narrating the lives of women both famous and obscure, Westview's "Lives of American Women" series populates our national past more fully and more richly. Each story told is that not simply of an individual but of the era in which she lived, the events in which she participated, and the experiences she shared with her contemporaries. Some of these women will be familiar to the reader; others may not appear at all in the history books that often focus on the powerful, the brilliant, or the privileged. But each of these women is worth knowing. American history comes alive through their personal odysseys.

—Carol Berkin

ACKNOWLEDGMENTS

My first thank-you goes to Carol Berkin, Presidential Professor at Baruch College CUNY and the CUNY Graduate Center (retired), scholar, author, professor, sister, colleague, comrade, coauthor, and editor who first suggested I write on Shirley Chisholm. Carol's generosity is equaled only by her brilliant, clever, and insightful writing; her sense of humor; her loyalty to friends; and her love for Johnny Depp. Marwa Amer, who was the manager of the Shirley Chisholm Project of Brooklyn Women's Activism from 2009 to 2011, has provided me with so many essential research documents, but more important, she has given me insights into the subject of women in the black freedom struggle. Stephanie Golden, a dear friend, writer, and editor, guided this work. A big thank-you to Susan Brownmiller for all her writings on Chisholm and for introducing me to Shola Lynch. Finally, I was so fortunate to work with project editor Carolyn Sobczak, who meticulously and ever so patiently worked with me at the last editing and footnoting stages of the manuscript.

Colleagues at Brooklyn College, Shirley Chisholm's alma mater, have been invaluable in their support. Two Brooklyn College presidents, Christoph Kimmich, who retired in 2009, and our current president, Karen Gould, have encouraged the project, both intellectually and materially. Thanks to Deborah Shanley, dean of the School of Education, who found ways to get me reassigned time for writing, encouraged me, and prodded me to finish. I am indebted to Marianne Labatto and Beth Evans, archivist and research librarians, respectively, at the Brooklyn College Library. What would I have done without their ability to find that document, that citation, that way to download JStor articles? I extend grateful thanks to my colleagues in the Women's and Gender Studies Program, Prudence Cumberbatch, Lynda Day, Namita Manohar, and Jeanne Theoharris, as well as to colleagues in the Secondary Education Department, Education, School Psychology/Counseling and Leadership and Childhood, BiLingual and Special Education Department, David Forbes, Sonia Murrow, Priya Parmer, Karel Rose, Jessica Seigel, and Peter Taubman. Other Brooklyn College faculty, Gunja Sen Gupta, Nancy Romer, and Jocelyn Wills, have been so supportive of this work. Lois Biesky, Ernesto Moro, and Marla Schreibman, also at Brooklyn College, have helped me find friends and colleagues of Chisholm to interview. Gwen Kay, SUNY Oswego, and Shannon Frystak, East Stroudsberg University, read the manuscript and provided me with important thoughtful suggestions.

Brooklyn College and the City University of New York have provided me with important external support. The Brooklyn College President's Office and Kimberly Phillips, dean of the School of Humanities and Social Science, have been both supportive and generous. Provost William Tramantano's 2012 Reassigned Time Award, two CUNY Diversity Grants (2008–2009, 2011–2012), a Brooklyn College TOW Travel Grant (2008), and two Professional Staff Congress (PSC CUNY) grants (2009–2010, 2010–2011) gave me needed reassigned time, plus funds for travel, research, and writing.

Archivists, librarians, and curators in Barbados opened many doors—Elizabeth Watson and Margaret Iton at the University of the West Indies, Cave Hill Library; Annette Smith at the National Library Service; David Williams, director of the National Archives; and Allissandra Cummins at the Barbados Museum and Historical Society—as well as the Mount Holyoke College Library Archives and Special Collections, Manuscripts.

Thanks also to the New York State Archives, Documentary History Project, and the New York State Council for the Humanities for their generous grants that furthered research on this book.

Thanks to Shola Lynch, not only for her award-winning documentary on Shirley Chisholm but for giving her entire collection of Chisholm materials to the Chisholm Archive. Jim Pitts's donation has been an extraordinary contribution to our knowledge of Chisholm as well as Democratic Party political activism in the 1970s. Both are part of the Chisholm Archive and are on exhibit once a year.

Special thanks to Rosalind Baxandall, Martha Biondi, Eileen Boris, Tammy Brown, Anastasia Curwood, Zinga Fraser, Jo Freeman, Julie Gallagher, Josh Guild, Melissa Harris-Perry, Kemille Jackson, Joyce LeeAnn Joseph, Iris Lopez, Premilla Nadasen, Brian Purnell, Barbara Ransby, and Beverely Guy Sheftall for their support, their critical comments, their incredibly useful suggestions, their inspired writing, and their activism. Manning Marable was the first person I went to about the Shirley Chisholm Project, and I keep his words of advice and encouragement close to my heart.

My friend Carolyn Umlauf, who is lucky not to be an academic, had to listen to me on our summer-morning walks go on and on about Chisholm. I am so blessed to have such a dear friend.

My two daughters, Jessie Winslow and Samantha Winslow, had to endure two summer vacations while I was getting the chapters written. I exhausted their patience as I begged for help learning how to navigate all the developments in technology. Much as I would rather join them biking, kayaking, hiking, beachcombing, movie-going—even shopping—they understood that I needed to stay inside and write, write, write. Thank you.

Introduction

Shirley Chisholm was both an ordinary and an extraordinary woman. The daughter of working-class Caribbean immigrants living in Bedford-Stuyvesant, Brooklyn, she was a churchgoer, teacher, and community activist. She ran for the presidency of the United States at a time when most African American women were domestics, teachers, or nurses; African Americans in the South had just been enfranchised, and American women did not enjoy the same rights as men.

This biography situates her remarkable narrative in the context of the tremendous social upheavals that took place in the post–World War II United States. Chisholm's life and legacy are the story of twentieth-century urban America. They broaden our perspective on the role African Americans, immigrants, and women played in shaping both the politics and the institutions of the country. Probably more than any other individual, Chisholm is representative of the 1945–1980 period, when women and underrepresented minorities— African Americans, Latinos, and immigrant Americans—came to the forefront of public life, including, for the first time, as elected officials on the national stage. Her audacious run for the US presidency in 1972 opened the country's eyes to the possibility that a woman or a person of color (even a woman of color) could be a political leader— even president of the United States.

This biography ends, for all intents and purposes, in 1972, after Chisholm lost her bid for the US presidency. In hindsight, one can see that although 1972 was the high point of her political career, it also marked the beginning of the decline of the urban liberal politics of Lyndon Johnson's Great Society—politics Chisholm embraced. Richard Nixon's election in 1968 and the subsequent collapse of liberal politics led to the election of Ronald Reagan in 1980. The repudiation of the 1960s Great Society reversed everything Chisholm supported and represented, in particular its social welfare legislation and the electoral and legislative victories that resulted from the civil rights and women's liberation movements.

Chisholm's narrative could be described as the quintessential "American Dream" story: a struggling African American working-class woman and daughter of Caribbean immigrants, who studiously applied herself and obtained a first-rate education through the public school system. Through hard work, discipline, and dedication, she became a teacher, a day-care worker, a local elected official, and then a national politician. She broke racial and gender barriers every step of her way. But, extraordinary as each triumph may be, these victories are only one part of her story. Chisholm's successful political career came about as a result of the great social movements of the twentieth century—including some outside the United States.

Her strong sense of identity was nurtured in Barbados, where as a young girl she was raised by a powerful, hardworking, stern, but loving grandmother and aunt during the island's struggle for independence from British colonial rule. In Brooklyn she had to navigate an unfamiliar if not hostile neighborhood, school system, and political machine, again during a period of great demographic, social, and political turmoil. She was schooled in the early black struggles of the late 1940s and '50s. Her Bedford-Stuyvesant neighborhood teemed with African Americans, people from the Caribbean, Puerto Ricans, Italians, and Jews, all involved in shifting social and political agendas, alliances, and battles. From her first foray into local politics, Chisholm learned how to successfully navigate these complicated waters.

Once on the political stage as a "first"—the first African American woman from Brooklyn elected to the New York State Legislature, the first African American woman elected to Congress, and then the first African American woman to make a run for the Democratic Party nomination for president—she found she had to fight constantly against the racial and gender prejudices of everyone around her. The media, the Congressional Black Caucus (CBC), and civil rights and feminist leaders often dismissed, underestimated, or patronized her. She held her ground, insisting that she was her own person—"Unbought and Unbossed" was her trademark slogan. But the world of electoral and legislative politics in the United States is one of compromise, and Chisholm found that despite maintaining a fiercely independent political persona, she also had to toe the party bosses' line in order to pursue her political agenda.

Reading Chisholm's campaign speeches, interviews, public pronouncements, and interviews, it is clear that her political positions then were—and even more so now are—strikingly radical. Her support for social justice, feminism, radical Black Nationalists, students, and prisoners fighting injustice, as well as her opposition to US foreign policy, places her left of center and certainly outside the politics of the Democratic Party today. Yet she chose not to participate in the social justice, civil rights, antiwar, or women's demonstrations, instead staying within the confines of the electoral political process. She was a pragmatic, strategic, and practical politician who pursued her political agenda by working within the Democratic Party, from local district politics to Washington, DC. Her presidential run was not as utopian a project as many of her detractors claimed. Chisholm had every reason to believe she was the best possible candidate, as she was confident of her ability to harness the energy and enthusiasm of newly enfranchised and empowered voters. She was certain that she could create a political coalition that could win delegate votes in the state primaries—and she did. She did not run for president just to make a political point. Her strategy was to bring her delegates to the Miami convention so that they could then use their delegate strength to bring progressive change to the Democratic Party.

Chisholm was like many strong feminist women of color who came before her and followed her. She was complicated. The stories she tells about herself, not surprisingly, put her in a positive light. In her two autobiographies, there are inconsistencies and significant gaps in her narratives. But she could be self-critical, especially when looking back at her 1972 election campaign. Although she was certainly a trailblazer—a "first"—she was also much more. A charming, flirtatious woman who loved to dance and an inveterate catalog shopper, she was described as one of the best-dressed women on the Hill. She was proud of her intellect, debating skills, and fluency in Spanish. She also had a wicked sense of humor and was a brilliant mimic of congressmen and even presidents. Her Brooklyn and Washington congressional staffs loved working with her and to this day remain loyal to her memory. She was a mentor and role model to the next generation of African American women leaders, including reproductive-rights activist Loretta Ross, CNN analyst Donna Brazile, and Congresswomen Barbara Lee and Eleanor Holmes Norton. Chisholm's 1972 presidential candidacy was a revelation to sixteen-year-old Anita Hill, who remembered that, "having that face, that strong voice, someone who looked like me—that mattered." At the end of her presidential campaign, she expressed her optimism and confidence in the American story: "We can become a dynamic equilibrium, a harmony of many different elements, in which the whole will be greater than all its parts and greater than any society the world has seen before. It can still happen. I hope I did a little to make it happen. I am going to keep trying to make it happen as long as I am able."[1]

1

Barbados

Shirley Anita St. Hill Chisholm was born in Brooklyn, on November 30, 1924, an American citizen, but she always saw herself as a Barbadian American. Just as the history of Barbados is inextricably linked to the history and development of the United States from its colonial beginnings to the present day, Chisholm could not separate the Bajun from the American. Barbados and Brooklyn formed her character, intellect, political and social awareness, self-confidence, and daring.

Barbados was connected to Britain's thirteen colonies in the North, later the United States, from the beginning of the English settlements. It was the first port of call for British ships sailing from either African or English ports to North America. The majority of slaves who came to the thirteen colonies had been "seasoned," or, more accurately, broken, in Barbados before being transported north. Close links were established between Barbados and the Carolinas when in 1670 a permanent colony was established in what is known today as Charleston, South Carolina. Many prominent Barbadian merchants and planters subsequently migrated to South Carolina, maintaining the Barbadian colonial connections. Barbadians contributed knowledge, lifestyle, and a sugar economy, along with place-names and a dialect. Barbados was a continual source of population for the American colonies. While slaves were sent mainly to the southern colonies, a smaller number of white bonded servants escaped, were indentured to northern colonial masters, or as freed people found a way to the North. Barbadian Jews moved to New York City.

Barbados and Barbadians were connected to the centrality of the history of the United States, in particular the patriotic folklore of the American Revolution—and some of its iconic figures. One Barbadian account claims that Crispus Attucks, remembered as the first American to die in the "Boston Massacre," where Massachusetts colonists fought for freedom from Britain, was originally from Barbados. In 1750 George Washington, first president of the United States, then nineteen years old, accompanied his elder half brother Lawrence, who was suffering from tuberculosis, to Bridgetown. Hoping that the warmer climate and cool breezes would cure Lawrence, the two men stayed for three months. While in Barbados the future first president contracted a mild case of smallpox. Barbados's climate failed to provide a cure for Lawrence Washington, who upon his return home died shortly thereafter. George Washington's trip to Barbados was his only venture outside what is now the United States.

The American Revolution further connected Barbados with the new Republic. At the end of the Revolutionary War, there was an exchange of families between the United States and Barbados. Loyalists, those colonists who supported the British Crown, moved to Barbados, while Barbadian sympathizers with the American Revolution settled in what became the United States. Some early Barbadians made lasting contributions to the economic and social life of the United States. One Barbadian family brought cotton plants to Georgia, which became the nucleus for the Sea Island cotton industry.[1]

Before Shirley Chisholm's parents arrived in Brooklyn, New York, other Barbadians played a role in the formation of the US Republic. Prince Hall, for example, an early Barbadian immigrant to the United States, made his mark as an active participant in the struggle for independence, abolition, and education. Born in Bridgetown, Barbados, on or about 1735 to an Englishman and a woman of African descent, he came to America in 1765. He was both an abolitionist and a Mason. Because of his organizing skill, a charter for the establishment of a lodge of African American Masons was issued on April 29, 1787. This authorized the organization in Boston of African

Lodge No. 459, a "regular Lodge of Free and Accepted Masons, under the title or denomination of the African Lodge," with Prince Hall as master. An outspoken abolitionist, he was one of eight Masons who signed a petition on January 13, 1777, requesting that Massachusetts's state legislature abolish slavery, declaring it as incompatible with the cause of American independence. In addition, he tried unsuccessfully to get free blacks and slaves to be able to enlist in the Continental army. He was later successful in urging Massachusetts to end its participation in the slave trade. He established the first school for African and African American children in his home in Boston in 1800.

In the twentieth century, economic changes were laying a new foundation that would continue the connection between Barbados and the United States. In 1904 the United States' construction of a canal across the Isthmus of Panama had profound repercussions for the Chisholm family, for Barbados, and for Brooklyn. From 1900 to 1925, more than 300,000 islanders, mainly from Barbados, left their homes to work on the Panama Canal or to immigrate to the States, the majority settling in Brooklyn. More than 10,000 Barbadian men, including Chisholm's grandfather, having never worked on anything but sugarcane fields, threw off the yoke of planter domination to build the Panama Canal. For the first time in their lives, they earned cash—"Panama Money," which was sent home, enabling village life to continue. Men were also paid in "Panama Gold." Muriel Forde, Chisholm's sister, who lives in Barbados today, recalls that "some of the very old women here in Barbados you see now, you'll see a gold ring on their finger and they say it's Panama Gold."[2] Chisholm's grandfather sent money to his daughter Ruby so that she could go to the United States. Ruby Seale, who was born in Christchurch, Barbados, in 1901, arrived in New York City aboard the SS *Pocone* on March 8, 1921.

Charles Christopher St. Hill, Chisholm's father, was born in British Guiana, now the independent nation of Guyana. Orphaned by age fourteen, Charles St. Hill and his brother began an odyssey that first took them to Barbados and then to Antilla, Cuba, for a year and finally to the United States. They arrived in April 1923 as part of what has been described as the "West Indian wing of America's great migration north." In addition to the 2 million blacks who moved from the American South to northern cities in the early decades of the twentieth century, 300,000 people, like St. Hill, came from the English-speaking Caribbean, looking for work and safety. The majority of these immigrants were from Barbados, and their destination was most often Brooklyn. From 1900 to 1920, the borough's black population doubled, and by 1930 16 percent of this population had come from the Caribbean.[3]

Although St. Hill was born in Guiana, he always considered himself a Barbadian. Like the majority of Barbadians, St. Hill settled in Brooklyn and found work and a wife. He and Ruby Seale had known each other slightly in Barbados, and they became reacquainted at one of Brooklyn's many Bajun social clubs. The two married after a strict traditional courtship. Children followed quickly: Shirley in 1924, Odessa in 1925, and Muriel in 1927. A fourth daughter, Selma, would follow in the midst of the Great Depression.

The St. Hill parents considered themselves American Barbadians, which meant they raised their children as Barbadians. The key characteristics of Barbadian Americans were discipline, thrift, hard work, and ambition. According to Chisholm, other islanders referred to Barbadians as "black Jews." In addition to these Barbadian characteristics, they were fiercely proud of their heritage, often bragging that Barbados was the first country in the English-speaking Caribbean to emancipate their slaves. Barbadians had two things in mind when they came to Brooklyn. The first was to secure a good education for their children. The people most respected in the Barbadian community were the parents whose children excelled in school. And the second, as Paule Marshall so brilliantly wrote in *Brown Girl, Brownstones,* a pathbreaking coming-of-age novel about a close-knit community of Barbadian immigrants in Brooklyn, was to own a home—a brownstone home. The St. Hills made sure their children did well in school, and finally in 1945 Charles and Ruby could afford a brownstone home. Muriel St. Hill Forde, who lived in the family's brownstone for thirty-two years, remembers that "the home is still there. We've been there for fifty-eight years . . . and if anybody asks me where my home is, I still think of that home as my home in Brooklyn." Muriel recalls with satisfaction that their parents "had achieved their ambitions: a home and education. That's what they wanted."[4]

But in the mid-1920s, the dream of a home and a good education was just that: a dream. The unprecedented prosperity of that decade—the booming economy, the expansion of industries—was not enjoyed by the majority of West Indians in Brooklyn. Charles was an unskilled laborer and could not secure factory work. Instead, he had to settle for a low-paying job as a baker's helper. Although Ruby was a skilled seamstress, she could not hold down a job in a textile factory because of her three rapid pregnancies. With no affordable nursery schools or day care, Ruby could not work outside the home. All she could do to contribute to the household economy was take in sewing. But as the girls got older, the diminutive Ruby found it impossible to manage both this work and three demanding children. Facing the reality of their situation, the St. Hills began to talk about sending their daughters to live temporarily on their maternal grandmother's farm in Barbados. Returning to the island was not an option for Charles and Ruby, for the economy there was far worse than in Brooklyn.

In November 1929 plans were made for Ruby, the three St. Hill daughters, and four cousins to sail on the *Vespress*. Trunks were packed and sent ahead to the docks. But five days before the scheduled departure, Ruby announced that they were not going to board that ship. A determined woman, Ruby got on the subway, the seven children in tow, and made her way to the ship line's booking office to rebook their passage, this time on the *Vulcana*. A day into their sea voyage, Ruby learned that the *Vespress* had sunk. From that moment on, Charles never questioned his wife's intuition.

The trip to Bridgetown, the capital of Barbados, took nine long seasick days. After making their way through customs and health inspections, the family boarded a rickety bus that took them along the dusty dirt roads to Vauxhall, the Seale family's village. Emmeline Seale, their grandmother, was waiting for the bus. She was "a tall, gaunt erect Indian looking woman with her hair knotted on her neck," Chisholm later recalled, adding, "I did not know it yet, but this stately woman with a stentorian voice was going to be one of the few persons whose authority I would never dare to defy."[5] After hours of embraces and chatter, the children were taken for baths in a galvanized tub in their grandmother's backyard. Then, utterly exhausted, they went to bed. Ruby stayed with her daughters for six months, helping them adjust to their new life. Then she returned to Brooklyn. She would not see her children for six years.

Their grandmother was the matriarch of the family, but she did not raise the children. She worked as a domestic for a British family. Her hours were long, and she often walked to work, leaving at sunup and not returning until nine or ten at night. Because of this Ruby's nineteen-year-old sister, Myrtle, cared for the seven children. On Saturdays they would go with their aunt Myrtle to the village market to sell their vegetables and bargain for kitchenwares. Sunday was devoted to religious observances. Granny Seale would lead the family to the local Methodist church; everyone dressed in their Sunday best. After a long service, the Seales would return home for a big dinner—and then head back to church for more song and prayer. Later in life Chisholm would attribute much of her success to the deep faith first instilled in her in Barbados.

The grandmother's large house sat on a plot that provided the family's food: sweet potatoes, yams, corn, tomatoes, and root vegetables. The waters around the island provided abundant seafood, including the Barbadian staple, flying fish. The children were all expected to do chores on the farm, and these including feeding and caring for the chickens, turkeys, and ducks as well as goats, sheep, and cows that provided milk. Whereas the Barbadian Seales saw these animals as livestock and food, the urban Brooklyn children viewed them as pets. They became quite upset when, for one Christmas dinner, a favorite turkey showed up as the main course. Soon enough, though, the seven children became accustomed to Bajun attitudes and life.

Life at their grandmother's was not all chores and church. The azure blue and crystal-clear water of the Caribbean was just a short walk from the farm. Together, the family would strip naked, swim in the water, and roll in the sand. The greatest punishment Granny Seale could mete out was to take away time at the beach.

Ruby Seale wanted her daughters educated in Barbados, for she believed the school system there would provide a more rigorous education than the public schools in Brooklyn. Here, there was no kindergarten, there was no play time, and the curriculum focused intensely on reading and writing, although students were also expected to study arithmetic, drawing and needlework, geography, and British history. There were also classes in religious and moral instruction, personal hygiene, domestic economics, and vocational training. Each day began with the singing of "God Save the King" and "Rule Britannia," a reminder that they were all colonial subjects of Great Britain. Strict discipline was enforced throughout the school day.

Five days a week, Aunt Myrtle walked all seven children across the road to the one-room schoolhouse that also served on the weekend as the village Methodist church. A school day lasted eight hours, from eight to four. The 125 students read their lessons aloud, and every child had a blackboard slate and a piece of chalk to practice penmanship and addition. In Barbados, Chisholm noted, teachers and parents were allies against the students. Few parents opposed the common use of corporal punishment, and Chisholm recalls that she got her fair share of floggings. She never complained. And in her autobiography, she credits her ability to speak and write to the strict British-style education of her childhood. Her Barbadian education also contributed to her sense of racial pride. Her schooling was remarkable in that it was run by black administrators, and she was taught by black teachers—something she would never experience as a student or educator in Brooklyn.

The Barbados of 1928 was not quite the idyllic paradise Chisholm describes in her autobiography. It was an impoverished island, dominated by a white planter class, the majority of its black inhabitants landless, unemployed or poorly paid, uneducated, and chronically sick. But during Shirley's years on Emmeline Seale's farm, black Barbadians were beginning to challenge both the planter class and the British Crown. Political disturbances swept through the countryside—there was widespread looting of potato fields and plantation supplies. Socialists, unionists, and anticolonial activists began organizing in the towns and countryside. The men in the villages went into Bridgetown, the center of political organizing and social unrest, to seek employment; women went into town to sell their wares. Shirley's uncle Lincoln worked for a Bridgetown newspaper and had to have been involved in or at least aware of the tremendous social protest.

During her years on Granny Emmeline's farm, Shirley St. Hill developed a strong sense of self. She was raised by two strong, hard-working women, her grandmother and aunt, which no doubt shaped her later feminist consciousness. Living through the early years of the struggle for the modern Barbadian nation gave her an understanding of the need to stand up and fight for one's principles, self-respect, as well as independence from oppressive and racially unjust relationships—whether personal or imbedded in economic or social relationships. And despite the dominance of wealthy whites and the British government, she had other daily role models in her teachers, the ministers, the tradespeople, newspaper editors, police, and even politicians who looked like her and her family, giving her a strong sense of racial pride and identity. "Granny gave me strength, dignity, and love," Chisholm told the *New York Times* in 1972. "I learned from an early age that I was somebody. I didn't need the black revolution to teach me that."[6] Gloria Steinem, Chisholm's friend and sister activist, suggested, in 2008, that Shirley's regal bearing and habit of speaking of herself in the third person, for which she would later become famous, "may have developed because a little bit of those British queenly images . . . rubbed off."[7]

2

Brooklyn

By 1933 the St. Hill family in Brooklyn was suffering the consequences of the 1929 stock market crash. Although many Americans endured poverty, joblessness, and often homelessness during the Depression, African Americans, and especially unskilled African American laborers like Charles St. Hill, fared the worst. In spite of the family's hard work and frugality, they could not save any money. The birth of their fourth daughter, Selma, put more strain on the family finances, as it made working difficult for Ruby St. Hill. Nevertheless, the St. Hills missed their other daughters so much that they decided to bring them back from Barbados. When ten-year-old Shirley St. Hill arrived on March 19, 1934, she had only dim recollections of her birthplace, little knowledge of Brooklyn's place in the world, and of course no idea how its history would shape her own future development. Young Shirley had just been transported from a nurturing, sheltered rural way of life to an urban world dominated by hierarchies of class, race, gender, and ethnicity. Just as her Bajun experience shaped Chisholm's worldview, her life in Brooklyn gave her the context for her future political philosophy and her electoral ambitions.

By the end of the nineteenth century, Brooklyn was the most populous borough in New York City. Between 1900 and 1920, its population rose to 2.5 million, and the number of citizens of color tripled to almost 70,000. Much of its population growth came from the two wings of the Great Migration—the movement of some

2 million blacks out of the American South to cities in the Midwest, Northeast, and West, and the emigration of 300,000 people from the English-speaking Caribbean. By 1930 16 percent of Brooklyn's black population had come, like the St. Hills, from the Caribbean.

Ruby Seale St. Hill and her daughters Shirley, Muriel, and Odessa arrived in Brooklyn on a cold March day. For the young Shirley, Brooklyn was an alien and terrifying place. First and foremost, it was cold. It was cold outside and it was cold inside, for the St. Hills lived in a four-room cold-water railroad flat, heated only by a coal stove in the kitchen. The family never used their parlor in the winter because it could not be heated. When their mother left the apartment to go shopping, the girls would stay in bed all day, just to keep warm. Throughout her life, Chisholm commented on her fear of the cold.

The St. Hills now lived at 110 Liberty Avenue in the Brownsville section of Brooklyn. Chisholm was initially confused and frightened by her neighborhood. She missed the freedom and space she enjoyed in Barbados. Her parents constantly warned her never to talk to strangers. In Barbados there were no strangers—everyone knew everyone. Cars, subways, and buses terrified her. She could not get used to walking on sidewalks, and to avoid the hustle of crowds she would walk in the streets. It took her a while to navigate her neighborhood. In her mind, all the streets looked the same, and she often got lost while doing errands for her family. In her autobiography, she described one incident when she thought she had a route to a particular store memorized, but then her designated landmark disappeared, and she got lost. "Things didn't change that way in Barbados," she wrote. "The village shoemaker's shop, for example, had been in the same place for generations."[1]

In the 1930s, Brownsville was a heavily Jewish neighborhood of poor and run-down apartments. With more than two hundred thousand people—including African Americans, Afro-Caribbeans, Italians, Puerto Ricans, and a small number of Syrians—all dwelling in its 2.19 square miles, it was the most densely populated district in Brooklyn. The borough's black neighborhoods were the most blighted and decaying; a local community study found that black Brooklynites occupied "the worst slum houses in excessively disproportionate numbers to their total population." Another study of a particularly impover-ished five-block area in Brownsville revealed the highest rates of infant mortality in all of Kings County.[2] Yet in her autobiography, Chisholm simply described her neighborhood this way: "Today we might call it a 'ghetto.' Its residents would have laughed at the word. Some of them were first generation Jews from central and Eastern Europe, and they knew the difference. They had come from real ghettos."[3]

But Brownsville's main streets were far from dismal. They teemed with life and were a refuge from and contrast to the grim housing conditions. The open-air market on Belmont Avenue was alive with shoppers looking for bargains. Shopkeepers, selling all varieties of ko-sher food, spoke to customers in Yiddish, and Jewish life and culture dominated the neighborhood, which boasted seventy Orthodox syn-agogues. Every Friday night and on Jewish holidays, the streets of Brownsville were hushed. After sunset on the Sabbath eve, only the flickering lights of candles could be seen from the tenement windows. But on Sunday, the streets came alive: carpenters, painters, electri-cians, and masons assembled on the corner of Pitkin and Stone Ave-nues, gossiping or complaining about their last job while they waited for the next contractor to hire them.

The neighborhood had both a long history of racial and religious tolerance and a rich tradition of radical social protest. Many of the St. Hills' Jewish neighbors were actively involved in the revitalization of housing for everyone in the neighborhood. Their concern for resi-dents of any race or religion led one New Deal emergency housing and mortgage agency to label them "communistic." Although this charge was unfounded, Brownsville had elected Socialists to the New York State Assembly in the years between 1915 and 1921. And in 1936, the American Labor Party, an organization founded by labor leaders and former members of the Socialist Party, ran a successful campaign to elect a candidate from Brownsville to the New York State Assem-bly. Brownsville had also been home to the first family-planning and birth-control clinic in America, founded by feminist and birth-control pioneer Margaret Sanger in 1916. Throughout her adult life, Chisholm embodied the best of her district: progressive politics, outspoken fem-inism, and support for the aspirations of ethnic and racial minorities.

The progressive spirit of the neighborhood could also be seen in the friendships the St. Hill family formed. Most of the St. Hill girls' playmates were Jewish. In all of Chisholm's later writings and speeches, she would reflect on the good relationship Bajuns enjoyed with their Jewish neighbors. In spite of the poverty of their family and their neighborhood, the St. Hill family found amusements. Shirley and her sisters marveled at the Brooklyn cinemas, an experience unknown in the islands. For ten cents the girls could attend Saturday matinees, staying through shows often after their dinnertime, only to be dragged out by their scolding mother. In the summers, Ruby and her sister Violet Jones would pack a picnic lunch and take the three St. Hill girls and Aunt Violet's four boys on the bus or subway to Jones Beach or Coney Island.

Movie theaters and beaches were welcome excursions, but education remained a central priority. Shirley's first experience in an American school was PS 84 on Glenmore Avenue. For the first time in her life, she would encounter hierarchies in the public schools, based on class, race, and gender—hierarchies she would encounter and struggle against the rest of her life. In every respect, her experiences in Brooklyn's public schools prepared her for her political career. In the 1930s, the leadership of Brooklyn public schools was one of the whitest in the nation; there were only a few black teachers and fewer black administrators. Her experiences navigating the challenges of racism in the Brooklyn public school system were in stark contrast to the progressive and communal spirit of her neighborhood. Having gone to a one-room schoolhouse in Vauxhall, Barbados, Shirley was awed at the thought that she was attending one of eighty-four elementary schools in just one of New York's five boroughs. But PS 84 was so overcrowded that the school day had to be truncated, and the St. Hill girls were assigned to a morning session. The school reflected the makeup of the district: it was about 80 percent white, and most of the students were Jewish. All of the teachers were white and Jewish as well. This was a totally different and discomfiting experience for a young black girl, having been used to a school with black teachers and students. Yet being in a racial minority did not seem to bother Chisholm at the time. Perhaps reflecting that in the absence of a visible militant black movement in Brooklyn, she could write that "the race line was not drawn in the same way it is today."⁴

One might argue that young Shirley's struggle against injustice began in the public schools. Her first term began disastrously. Instead of putting her in the sixth grade, the school administration placed her in the third grade. They had been satisfied with her reading and writing skills, but her lack of knowledge about US history and geography put her in a classroom with children much younger than herself. Bored and unhappy with what she saw as an unfair "demotion," Shirley became a discipline problem. She snapped rubber bands and threw spitballs, not only at her classmates but at her teacher as well. Fortunately, her third grade teacher realized what prompted this behavior and arranged for Shirley to be tutored. Within a year and a half, she had caught up with—and passed—her schoolmates her own age. From that point on, Shirley loved school, loved learning, and made up her mind to spend her life in the service of public education.

Like education, religion remained a significant factor in St. Hill family life. The family now belonged to the English Brethren Church, a small Quaker-like sect that had been established by West Indian immigrants. The family attended three separate services on Sundays with no minister and no formal service. Parishioners sat in a circle and spoke only when the spirit moved them. A head brother would lead the congregation in a hymn and amens. Chisholm hated the silences and chafed at not being allowed to whisper or giggle. But her mother was emphatic that the children would "grow up to be good Christians," and this strong religious upbringing stayed with Chisholm throughout her life.

In 1936 Ruby St. Hill told her husband they needed a larger apartment, one with heating. After much searching, they settled for a roomier, heated flat at 420 Ralph Avenue in the Bedford-Stuyvesant section of Brooklyn. This was the district that Shirley Chisholm would eventually represent, first as a state assemblywoman in Albany and then as a congresswoman for sixteen years. All that lay in the future; for twelve-year-old Shirley, this move to a new neighborhood opened her eyes to racial and ethnic hatred. It was in Bedford-Stuyvesant, she recalled, that she heard "racial slurs and epithets . . .

nigger, kike, Jew bastard, black son of a bitch. I was not used to black being used as a derogatory word."[5] The Bedford and Stuyvesant sections of central Brooklyn had historically been solid, residential, middle-class, and overwhelmingly white neighborhoods, with blocks and blocks of stately brownstone townhouses, beautiful churches, excellent public schools, and libraries. In 1939, just as tens of thousands of southern and Caribbean blacks were moving to Brooklyn, a subway line linking Harlem and Bedford-Stuyvesant was constructed, and African Americans began to leave overcrowded Harlem for this Brooklyn neighborhood. White residents reacted with hostility, fear, resentment, anger, and active discrimination. By the time the St. Hill family moved to Ralph Avenue, there had been almost a decade of racial segregation in the neighborhood churches and schools as well as civic and community organizations. In 1921 a Brooklyn klavern of the Ku Klux Klan enjoyed support from some of Brooklyn's less enlightened clergymen.

In her new neighborhood, Chisholm attended PS 28, where racial hostility came from both her classmates and her teachers. She then moved on to middle school at JHS 178. Because Ruby St. Hill was now once again employed, young Shirley became the head of the family during the school week. Every day she would walk to junior high school, and then at noon she picked up her sisters, who were still at PS 28, and took them home for lunch. After a spartan meal—usually no more than a glass of milk and a bun—Shirley would take her sisters back to PS 28 and return to her school. When school was over, she would again pick up her sisters and take them home. Today, one might describe the St. Hill daughters as latchkey children, returning from school to an empty home because a parent or parents were away at work. No doubt, Shirley's experiences caring for her sisters while her parents worked made her a lifelong champion of day care.

Shirley's experiences of poverty and racism made her fiercely determined to succeed in life. She had, after all, experienced poverty, in different situations—one rural, in Barbados, the other urban, in Brooklyn. The rural poverty of Barbados never seemed quite so harsh. The climate was warm, and there was always the beach. The St. Hills could eat fresh food from their grandmother's farm, and finally the racial stigma attached to poverty was far less than she experienced in Brooklyn. She carried with her memories of urban poverty, however: the stale breads and pastries, the shopping for inexpensive day-old vegetables, and the rarity of meat. She remembered that her mother, who worked as a domestic for white families, would often come home with leftover food and hand-me-down clothing. But Shirley also remembered the role her mother played in making her own success possible. She deeply admired her stern but loving mother, who, like Granny Emmeline, stressed the value of a good education. Despite her long workday, Ruby often did the girls' chores so they could concentrate on their homework, and every other Saturday she took her daughters to the local public library, where each was expected to check out three books. During those two weeks, their mother would ask questions about their reading, for she expected them to finish all three books before the next trip to the library. Each daughter had a dictionary, and Christmas gifts were usually books. Ruby also encouraged her daughters' interest in music, buying a second-hand piano for their apartment and finding money for Shirley to take music lessons. Chisholm's later advocacy of domestic workers' unions that could help these workers gain better benefits, wages, and working conditions arose directly from her mother's experiences.

But while young Shirley loved and admired her mother, she adored her father, idolizing his good looks and intelligence. Charles St. Hill finished only the fifth form in school—the equivalent of the fifth grade in the United States—but he was self-educated and well read. His daughter always believed he could have been a brilliant scholar had he been able to go to university. Shirley received most of her education about politics, labor, and black history at the kitchen table, listening to her father's stories about island politics and the struggle against British colonialism. Perhaps his words brought back memories of her time in Barbados during the anticolonial awakening. He was a proud follower of Marcus Garvey, a Jamaican publisher, journalist, entrepreneur, and orator who was a staunch proponent of Black Nationalism and Pan-Africanism. In 1916 Garvey settled in Harlem and established the Universal Negro Improvement Association (UNIA), which promoted black pride and black power. He founded the Black Star Line, part of the Back-to-Africa movement, which promoted the return of the African Diaspora to their ancestral lands. In nine years Garvey built the largest mass movement of people of African descent probably in the world. He and the UNIA had influenced the developing radical and black consciousness of Barbadian workers, and Garvey's political ideas remained rooted in the political consciousness of Charles St. Hill.

Charles instilled racial pride and self-confidence in his children. He was also a proud trade unionist who belonged to the Confectionery and Bakers International Union. Charles would come home from work and read aloud from the many union papers he brought. He was particularly proud to have been elected a union shop steward. He always shined his shoes and wore a suit and tie when he went to union meetings. "It was the first time in his life," wrote Shirley, "he had been given the recognition his talents deserved."[6] Just as Ruby Seale's life convinced Shirley to champion day care and the rights of domestic workers, her father's experience convinced her that unions could enhance workers' standard of living and quality of life. But most important, Charles St. Hill took his daughter seriously. He raised her to value education, political activism, public service, and fearlessness when acting on one's convictions.

In 1939 the St. Hills' fortunes changed for the better. Charles got a new job as a janitor, and the family was able to move into a rent-free six-room apartment. The added income meant that Ruby Seale did not have to go outside the home to work and could be there to greet her children when they arrived from school. Even better, Shirley had been accepted to the prestigious Girls' High School, a historically and architecturally notable public secondary school located at 475 Nostrand Avenue, within walking distance of the new apartment. Girls' High was built in 1886 and is the oldest public high school building in New York City still standing. Today it is a designated New York City landmark. According the *New York Times,* it was "the ambition of every Brooklyn girl . . . to enter the Girls High School where she may enjoy the advantages of an advanced education and be prepared for college."[7] The girls were offered courses in Latin, Greek, German, French, botany, zoology, physics, chemistry, astronomy, physiology, psychology, algebra, geometry, calculus, economics, and ancient, medieval, and modern history, and classes in the "literary masterpieces, both American and English." Young women came from all parts of Brooklyn to attend the school, and whereas the Bedford-Stuyvesant neighborhood was all black, the school was half African American, half white.

Shirley excelled at Girls' High. She earned a medal for her proficiency in French, and, at a time when few students of color were elected to student offices, she was chosen vice president of Junior Arista, a girls' honor society. She also developed a taste for fun. Even though her parents, especially her mother, were very strict, young Shirley began her adolescent rebellion playing jazz on the piano, allowing boys to walk her home from school, and even allowing herself to be kissed on occasion. Her father would try to convince Ruby to adapt to the ways of their new country. "Ruby, you must remember these are American kids, not island kids," he would plead. "Charles," Ruby would respond, "We've got to be strict on them if we want them to grow up to be something."[8]

Chisholm graduated from Girls' High in 1942, and even though she was offered scholarships to attend Vassar and Oberlin Colleges, her family could not pay for room and board at an out-of-town school. Somewhat reluctantly, she applied to Brooklyn College and was admitted. Tuition was free; she could live at home and travel to her classes on the subway. In her autobiography Chisholm wondered whether, if she had gone to Oberlin or Vassar, she would have become a pampered upper-class African American wife, riding around in limousines and putting on airs. In any case, she never regretted her choice: "Brooklyn College," she wrote, "changed my life."

Brooklyn College was established in 1930 by the New York City Board of Higher Education. In 1932 the college moved to the Flatbush section of Brooklyn, and classes began on the new campus five years later. This college, one of the largest city-run institutions, established a reputation for being academically challenging. In the 1940s, it was difficult for women to be admitted because of two commonly held prejudices of the time: first, the belief that women were not as smart as men, and second, that women went to college primarily to find husbands. Thus, the grade point average required for a woman to enter Brooklyn College was 83.5 percent; for men it was 79 percent.

A nervous Shirley St. Hill entered Brooklyn College in the fall of 1942. Even though she had lived in Brooklyn for almost a decade and excelled in high school, she now saw herself as a sheltered, naive student. She was awestruck at the sight of thousands of apparently confident students rushing to classes, meetings, the library, or the cafeteria, chatting with friends and professors. Because the college was tuition free and described as "a subway campus," Shirley expected more African American students. Instead, she found herself one of approximately sixty black students out of a total graduate and undergraduate population of ten thousand. The college president, Dr. Harry Gideonse, was white, and so was the entire upper-level administration. Chisholm chose to major in sociology, a department whose faculty was all white and all male. The student council was also all white, as were the staffs of the college yearbook, the *Broeklundian,* and the radical student newspaper, the *Vanguard,* as well as the official college publication, the *Pulse.* For the first time in her life, Shirley was indeed Langston's Hughes's "raisin in the sun."

Shirley concentrated solely on her studies her first year. She was very aware that she had a great responsibility to her family to do well. Her parents were very proud of their college daughter, but they continued to be strict, not allowing her to have a social life. She spent most of her time in the college library. Although she had planned to become an elementary schoolteacher, she took no education courses. Instead, she majored in sociology and minored in Spanish. Her decision to pursue a career in education was based upon her understanding of what opportunities existed for African American women in the 1940s. The fields of law and medicine were too expensive, and social work was not yet open to people of color.

Shirley excelled during her first year, which gave her the confidence to plunge into the myriad political activities taking place on campus. The nation was at war, and the campus was alive with political protest. A wide range of radical political clubs organized meetings, leafleted students, or assembled platforms to call attention to their particular cause. The first group Chisholm joined was the one all-black organization, the Harriet Tubman Society, founded in 1941. Almost every African American student was a member of this society, which organized a wide range of programs and speakers, including internationally renowned singer, actor, and political activist Paul Robeson and Adam Clayton Powell, the first African American elected to Congress from a northern state. He was the most important black elected official, representing Harlem, the political, intellectual, and artistic capital of black America. Sitting in the cafeteria, members held discussions on black history and black leaders such as Harriet Tubman, W. E. B. DuBois, Frederick Douglass, and Mary McLeod Bethune. They circulated petitions to integrate the military and demanded black faculty and courses in African American history. In 1943 Shirley worked on the campaign of Georgina Pearl Graham, a Tubman Society member who unsuccessfully ran as an independent candidate for student government.

Shirley also loved the Debating Society, and within a short time it became her favorite extracurricular activity. She gained confidence as a persuasive public speaker; not surprisingly, her favorite debate subjects were discrimination and prejudice. Shirley later credited her experience with the Brooklyn College Debating Society for preparing her to be a powerful public speaker. She also joined the Political Science Club but was very critical of many of the members who thought of themselves as very progressive but consistently brought in speakers who spoke patronizingly about helping "the Negro because the Negro is limited."[9] Aware that women were rarely elected to student offices, Shirley also supported the campaigns for women candidates, black or white, painting posters, organizing rallies, and even speaking on a few occasions. She was equally pained that black students were not welcome in the social clubs, and so, with a group of women friends, she founded an organization called IPOTHIA, which stood for In Pursuit of the Highest in All. Her extracurricular activities also included joining the Brooklyn chapter of the National Association for the Advancement of Colored People (NAACP) and the Brooklyn Urban League as well as working at the Brooklyn Home for the Aged.

Shirley's political science professor Louis Warsoff was the first person to recognize her political potential. She affectionately called

Warsoff "Proffy," and he was the first white person Shirley trusted. They engaged in lengthy political discussions, and one day Professor Warsoff startled her by announcing, "You ought to go into politics." Surprised at what she thought was his naïveté, she replied, "Proffy, you forget two things. I'm black—and I'm a woman." He replied, "You really have deep feelings about that, haven't you?" Shirley's growing awareness of these "deep feelings," what one would describe today as race and gender consciousness, was a central legacy of her experience at Brooklyn College. This raised consciousness would be a motivating force throughout her political career. She was deeply aware—and resentful—of the fact that whites looked upon blacks as inferior and in need of white help. She chafed at the thought that because of her skin color, she was expected to be subservient to whites. She came to realize the deep-seated, extensive racism in US society.

Over time, college friends and associates other than Professor Warsoff came to her and suggested she become more involved in political struggles. When Chisholm graduated cum laude from Brooklyn College in 1946, she still planned to devote her life to the betterment of children. Yet Proffy's mentoring, coupled with her experiences at Brooklyn College, had planted the germ of political ambition. Aware that she was angry about the racism of American society, Shirley grew more resolved to "do something about the way whites treated my people." Although a career in politics was "hardly even a fantasy for me at the time," she vowed, "If I ever had a chance, somehow I would tell the world how things were as I saw them."[10]

3

All Politics Is Local

Shirley's parents were particularly proud of their daughters' graduations from Brooklyn College. Shirley's sister Muriel Ford graduated, also cum laude, the next year. They had achieved one of the main goals they had set forth for themselves and their daughters: to provide their children with an excellent education. In 1945 the St. Hills' fortunes had brightened. Charles St. Hill had worked overtime at a burlap bag factory during the war and was able to save ten thousand dollars. With that money, he bought a three-story house on Prospect Place in the Bedford-Stuyvesant neighborhood. The family lived there for the rest of their lives. That these two immigrants, one an unskilled laborer and the other a part-time domestic, could achieve both these cherished goals was no small feat. After the family moved in, Charles told his daughters, "Your mother and I have worked hard and we have accomplished our two goals in life." He then promised his daughters, "if you work hard and never lose sight of your goals, you can do the same."[1]

Upon graduation Shirley began looking for a job. She had her heart set on being an elementary schoolteacher but found herself being turned down for job after job, even for positions as a teacher's aide. She believed that white racism was the main reason she couldn't get hired. On one occasion, she traveled to Riverdale, an affluent residential neighborhood in the Bronx, for a job interview. Although she possessed all the stated qualifications, she knew it was unlikely that this school would hire an African American. When the school administrator told her that she did not possess the necessary qualifications, Chisholm angrily responded, "You are not looking for someone with more administrative experience. You didn't know I was black." After this rejection, she promised herself, "If the day would ever come that I had a platform, boy, white America would never forget me."[2]

Shirley faced aspects of age discrimination as well. Many of her interviewers could not believe that this tiny woman weighing ninety pounds was twenty-two years old. After too many unsuccessful job interviews, she finally exploded at one nursery school director, "Don't judge me by my size!" Finally, Eula Hodges of the Mount Calvary Child Care Center in Harlem was persuaded to employ her on a probationary basis. Soon she was hired permanently. Shirley worked at Mount Calvary for seven years, from 1946 to 1953.

Convinced that her vocation would be in early childhood education, Shirley enrolled in the master's degree program in early childhood at Columbia Teachers College. She worked at the day-care center during the day, attended night classes, and then took the long subway ride home back to Brooklyn. Weekends were devoted to studying, for she was determined to excel at whatever she did. She graduated with a master of arts in "Curriculum and Teaching—Childhood Education—Young Children" on June 7, 1951.

She also found time to fall in love. For most of Shirley's college years, she had little time to enjoy a social life of parties and dating. She was extraordinarily conscientious about her studies, and most of her free time was spent in the library or participating in a myriad of campus and extracurricular activities. Young men, who thought of Shirley as just an intellectual, interested only in the serious issues of the day, were surprised when she did show up at parties. They were even more amazed that not only did she love to dance, but she was great at it, even winning dance prizes. Throughout her career, at political gatherings or parties, Shirley was always the first on the dance floor and the last to leave.

During her Easter break in 1946, she took a job in a jewelry factory in Manhattan. Even though her strict mother had warned her to eat alone and not to speak to strangers, Shirley found herself being charmed by an older Jamaican man whom she never names. They began dating steadily even before she graduated from college and after five years, in spite of her mother's vehement opposition, became engaged. Almost immediately, the engagement unraveled disastrously. Shirley found out her fiancé was married, had a family in Jamaica, and was involved in fraudulent immigration, birth certificate, and blackmail schemes. Distraught, she broke off the engagement. Soon after, her ex-fiancé was arrested and deported by the Immigration and Naturalization Service.

Shirley was shattered by this experience. "I hated men and I always would," she vowed. She couldn't sleep or eat and even considered suicide. She was slim to begin with, but now her weight loss made her appear almost skeletal. Finally, the family doctor encouraged her to take a leave from school and work and visit family friends who owned a farm in New Jersey. There, surrounded by caring friends, she got plenty of fresh air, rest, good food, love, and comfort. Soon she was able to return to work at the day-care center and continue studying for her master's degree. But she remained convinced that as a consequence of the devastating love affair, her "future would be one of complete devotion to the profession of child welfare and early childhood education, and one of spinsterhood."[3]

As it turned out, though, she had already met the person she would soon marry. One evening, as she was running from class to a meeting, Conrad Chisholm stopped her, and they had a short conversation. Born in 1916 in Montego Bay, Jamaica, the fifth of twelve children, Conrad came to New York in 1946. He worked first in the garment industry and then as a short-order chef at the Automat. Eventually, he became a private investigator. Shirley thought this stocky, handsome man was nice, but at the time she was in love and engaged to another man. When Shirley went back to Teachers College, Conrad began to court her. He waited for her after class or after work. He visited her at her Brooklyn home, and Shirley's mother welcomed this suitor warmly. Over time Conrad's persistence and admiration of Shirley's intellect, drive, and ambition, as well as his kindness, won Shirley over. They were married in 1949 in a big West Indian wedding. Shirley was twenty-five years old. They rented a small house in Brooklyn, close to her parents. Throughout their marriage, Conrad was a behind-the-scenes supporter of his wife. Shirley wrote that he was never jealous of her fame, never wanted to share or hog the spotlight. He saw his job as both promoting and protecting his wife. They were a very close couple, sharing a love for theater, reading political biographies, and swimming. They vacationed in the Caribbean once a year. Their only disappointment was that Chisholm miscarried twice and they had no children. Shirley was very proud of her marriage to Conrad. "You always said Jamaican men want the best," Chisholm once teased her husband. "So you just had to marry a Bajun girl."

In 1953 she became the director of the Friend in Need Nursery in Brooklyn, then after a year assumed the directorship of the Hamilton-Madison Child Care Center in Manhattan. She worked there for five years, supervising a staff of twenty-four, caring for 130 youngsters between the ages of three and seven. She brought to this job her own experiences as a young child in Barbados, the knowledge from her graduate courses at Teachers College, the skills learned at Mount Calvary and as the director of the Friend in Need Nursery, as well as her own ideas about day care and early childhood education. She believed that if she could learn to read and write by age four, so could other children. Almost half of the youngsters at Hamilton-Madison were Puerto Rican. Chisholm insisted they learn English. But she knew that in order to be effective with Spanish-speaking children, she must learn their language as well. Chisholm's fluency in Spanish helped her succeed at the day-care center and was invaluable in her later political endeavors.

During Shirley's senior year at Brooklyn College, Cleo Skeete, Shirley's hairdresser, had introduced her to another man who became as important to her as her father and her husband. Wesley McDonald (Mac) Holder, one of Brooklyn's most influential politicians in the post–World War II years, became her political mentor and she his protégée. Later in her political life, Chisholm characterized her relationship with Holder as "like Gepetto . . . and I was Pinocchio." Sometimes referred to as "the sly old mongoose" or the "dean of black Brooklyn politics," Holder immigrated to Brooklyn from British

Guiana in 1920. Well educated with a degree in mathematics and a supporter of Garvey, he settled in Brooklyn, where he was the field secretary of the Universal Negro Improvement Association and African Communities (Imperial) League. He was briefly the editor of the *Amsterdam News,* the influential African American newspaper. Holder began his political career working for the Kings County attorney Samuel Lebowitz, the lawyer who in the early 1930s defended the young black men known as the Scottsboro Boys, nine young men who were wrongfully accused and convicted of rape in Alabama in a trial that had international repercussion for racism in the United States.

Shirley Chisholm's career in politics began when she joined the Seventeenth Assembly District (17AD) Democratic Club in Bedford-Stuyvesant while still in college. Party politics, and in Brooklyn this meant largely Democratic Party politics, worked through political clubhouses. The club's primary function was to support the party's candidate at election time. Nearly every Brooklyn neighborhood had a club, usually headed by a district leader, and that district leader had always been white and male. Members of different clubs gathered periodically to choose candidates for offices beyond their own assembly districts—for example, for Congress, judgeships, and state senators.

By the time Chisholm began attending Democratic Party club political activities, the struggle for greater black representation in New York City and New York State politics was well under way. According to Chisholm, her early experiences in the 17AD Democratic Club made it clear that the club did not reflect the aspirations and struggles of Bedford-Stuyvesant, a community overwhelmingly African American. Acutely aware of the club's racial politics, she commented on the unwritten rules that had blacks sitting on one side of the meeting room and whites on the other. Women were not present. She was disgusted that even though the district they represented was probably two-thirds black, the white politicians did all they could to oppose any black candidate for office. Rather than being intimidated by these gender and racial politics, Chisholm, undaunted, asked the white councilmen why trash was not picked up regularly in their neighborhood as it was in the white districts. Could politicians explain why Bedford-Stuyvesant does not have decent police protection?

Can Brooklyn's housing codes be enforced? Why do these politicians fail time and time again to deliver on their many promises? Their lack of answers only propelled Chisholm into further activism.

Chisholm's first political success was working with the women in the club. In 1944, while still in college, Chisholm had experienced gender exclusion and found herself promoting women's aspirations for political office. But once out of college and out in the world of work and politics, she became even more acutely aware of gender discrimination. She noticed that club leaders were men; the women, mainly wives of club members, were expected to fulfill traditional gender roles—to organize socials, raffles, and other fund-raising events. She was put in charge of collecting money for raffle tickets and was so successful that she immediately became a leader of the women's group. What she realized, and pointed out to the other women, was how the men were exploiting their labor by not giving them a proper budget for their work. Unlike the men who had money to carry out their political tasks and responsibilities, the women were expected to beg and borrow money to buy prizes and to pay for the cost of printing raffle books. Finally, the women spoke up at a political meeting, demanding recognition as well as money for their work. Chisholm had earned support from the club's women. This forced the men to treat Chisholm with greater respect. In fact, they elected her to the club's board of directors—no small accomplishment for a twenty-year-old black woman.

Chisholm provided pivotal leadership and mentoring for the women in the clubs. In a 2011 interview, Basil Paterson, a pivotal figure in New York State politics, a leading African American lawyer, political activist, and close friend and ally, commented on the difficulties women faced in Brooklyn politics in the 1950s:

> If you think being a woman is bad now, they were horrible then. Women were not included in meetings. It was unbelievable. You would go to an important meeting, and there are no women there. Women were always very active; they were the most members of the clubs, they prepared the food for functions they had, and they sold tickets to the affairs. They never ran for office. That's what

made Shirley Chisholm such a stellar light; Shirley proved to women that you didn't have to just prepare the food and sell the tickets; you could get out there and run for higher office. And you could be your own person.[4]

This initial experience in Brooklyn party politics contained lessons that were invaluable for the rest of her political career. She learned, to her disgust, that the established political parties existed to keep the powerful in power. The rank and file were expected not to "rock the boat," and one way to deal with "troublemakers" like Shirley was to try to co-opt them with positions of leadership. The political clubs were as hierarchical as the rest of American society: a few white men were the leaders, with the rank and file doing the menial jobs as doorbell ringers and envelope stuffers. The women were expected to be invisible at meetings but be responsible for fundraising and the club's social life. This was not the political activism of Chisholm's aspirations.

With Chisholm's support, Holder led the Brooklyn black insurgency that challenged the entrenched Democratic machine. This first local struggle educated Chisholm about the ins and outs of politics—local as well as national. In many respects, the events that took place in Brooklyn were similar to events taking place in a number of northern cities. In 1953 a political vacancy opened up on the Second Municipal Court, which was in the Bedford-Stuyvesant area. At that time, there were forty-nine civil judges in the Brooklyn courts—all white—even though much of the courts' work involved African Americans. Lewis S. Flagg Jr., a very well-respected attorney, black civic leader, and activist, had earlier expressed interest in the post. Black Brooklynites were enraged when the Democratic Party machine nominated a white judge. Not only did the Democrats pass over qualified black jurists like Flagg, but they brought in someone who did not even live in Bedford-Stuyvesant. Immediately, Holder challenged the Democratic Party machine by organizing the Committee for the Election of Lewis Flagg Jr.

The series of primary elections and caucuses held in Brooklyn, as well as throughout states in the United States, is part of the process by which candidates for political office are selected. Political parties and primary elections were never mentioned in the US Constitution, and as political parties developed so did this primary process. Some states, like New York, hold only primary elections; other states, such as Iowa, for example, hold caucuses, where instead of going to a polling booth, voters participate in a local event, organized by the political party, and choose their preferred candidate. Some states use a combination of caucus and primary. Because Brooklyn voted overwhelmingly Democratic in local, state, and national elections, the winner of the Democratic Party primary almost always prevailed on election day.

Shirley Chisholm was one of the leaders of this primary campaign. She threw herself into ringing doorbells, stuffing envelopes, raising money, knocking on doors, and going to community, church, and political meetings. She talked to people, hoping to convince them that it was possible to challenge the white establishment, as well as to elect an African American judge, and that the African American community did not owe the local Democrats their loyalty. Every prominent political, religious, and civic African American organization supported Flagg, regardless of political party affiliation. Their efforts—and hers—paid off. Flagg outpolled the white Democratic candidate, and with this primary victory secure he went on to be the first African American jurist in Brooklyn. Never again would the Democratic Party machine write off black Brooklyn.

Energized by Flagg's victory, and with Chisholm's help, Holder rechristened the election committee the Bedford-Stuyvesant Political League with the hopes of repeating Flagg's triumph. Chisholm described the BSPL as an insurgent political club, and she was proud to be one of the insurgents. The BSPL's mission was to "bring about fuller political representation of Negroes and to secure their full participation in the social and economic life of the community." In 1954, under the banner "Let's Make History Again," the BSPL ran a full slate of black candidates against the regular Democrats—candidates for Congress and for the New York State Legislature. Holder ran for district leader. But none of the candidates won. Although Holder and others ran for political office in the next years, the magic of the Flagg campaign was gone.

Chisholm was active in all these BSPL campaigns, but at the same time she was developing her own political point of view. She might have thought of herself as an insurgent, but she was also a savvy, pragmatic, and strategic political activist—a politician in the making. While she was actively campaigning for Flagg, organizing the BSPL, pushing voter registration, and supporting their insurgent candidates, she continued to attend the meetings of the traditional Seventeenth Assembly District Club. By straddling both fences, so to speak, she was positioning herself for her own future political campaigns.

In 1958, at thirty-four years of age, Chisholm was a prominent league activist, leading delegations to city hall and speaking at rallies. She was elected league vice president, and friends encouraged her to run for league president. At first she held back. Holder was more than her friend and mentor; he was the founder of the league. The odds of winning were slight, and the chances of making a lifelong enemy were great. Yet she finally agreed to run, and as expected she faced Holder's wrath. He accused her of being disloyal, of turning on the very person who had taught her everything about politics, and threatened her with political isolation. Aware of the risks she faced, she went ahead. As predicted, Holder waged a no-holds-barred campaign, using all his political skills and clout and calling in all favors, and as expected Chisholm lost the election. Her friendship and political alliance with Holder were broken. Their rift lasted ten years. Not surprisingly, the BSPL suffered as well. Its inability to replicate Flagg's success, plus the infighting over the leadership, weakened the organization, and it folded a few years later. But this struggle demonstrated Chisholm's ambition that was then so strong she was willing to go against her mentor, and no doubt steeled her for future campaigns.

Chisholm left the BSPL that same year, and soon after she left the 17AD Democratic Club. Fed up with politics and believing she had nowhere to go politically, she put her political ambitions on hold. She reflected on this political experience. Was she right to challenge the white men in the 17AD club? Was it politically smart to challenge her mentor, Wesley McDonald Holder? She had few regrets and was proud that she had at least tried to put herself forward. She had spent the past ten years as coffee maker, leafletter, canvasser, doorbell ringer, speech maker, and rally organizer. She did not want to be a lifelong rank and filer but a political leader, a mover and shaker in her own right. This local activism was her advanced degree, her training for statewide and then later national political campaigning.

During this time, her professional and personal life flourished. By 1959 she was a consultant to the New York City Division of Day Care in the Bureau of Child Welfare, supervising ten day-care centers, seventy-eight teachers, and thirty-eight other employees. She was in charge of establishing new centers as well as assessing the programs and activities of other day-care agencies. Her mission was to promote child care in New York City, and this meant endless meetings with political and community leaders, trying to convince them that the city's children needed more and better facilities. Her work in the schools as a teacher and as an administrator stayed with her always. Even though she is most famous for being a pioneering black elected official, Chisholm always saw herself first and foremost as a teacher.

She remained very close to her father, who had been her political confidant during the 17AD and BSPL struggles. Her marriage with Conrad was strong and loving. In spite of her disappointment at being childless, Shirley knew that she could have a full life, devoting her time to improving the lives of the children of others. She did not need politics. Always ambitious, she was confident she would make her mark in the field of day care.

4

Black Power

In the winter of 1960, Chisholm reentered Brooklyn politics—something that was bound to happen, given her deeply ingrained love of political activism. Her excitement about the social upheaval taking place in the United States convinced her that the challenges to racial segregation that began in the 1950s were only going to continue to shake up the nation. The year 1960 was indeed a momentous one, especially for African Americans. On February 1, four young African American men, in direct violation of southern segregation laws, sat down at the lunch counter inside the Woolworth's store in Greensboro, North Carolina. They refused to leave unless they were served the same as the white patrons. Within days students in other North Carolina towns launched their own sit-ins, and within weeks thousands of students throughout the South were engaged in nonviolent sit-ins, protesting segregation in all forms of public accommodation. The sit-in movement was but another phase in the burgeoning southern civil rights movement, which first made national headlines in 1954 with the Supreme Court decision *Brown v. Board of Education of Topeka,* which declared school segregation unconstitutional; then in 1955 after the brutal murder of Emmett Till, a young Chicago teenager, by Mississippians; and finally the Montgomery bus boycott. New names and faces—Rosa Parks, Dr. Martin Luther King Jr., Ella Baker, Diane Nash, James Farmer, Charles and Shirley Sherrod, and Fannie Lou Hamer—became leaders and spokespersons for this new surge of courage and militancy.

The civil rights movement shook the country, sparking a wave of activism that demanded the full realization of the promises of the Declaration of Independence. Millions of Americans, inspired by the political militancy of the civil rights activists, came to believe that their collective actions could affect issues that before had only been discussed behind the closed door of the political club, the courthouse, or the board room. Although there had been significant civil rights activism in Brooklyn before 1955, the massive involvement of hundreds of thousands of young people challenging the very structures of racism and southern apartheid inspired northern activists to continue the struggle in their neighborhoods.

The civil rights struggle in the North, and particularly in Brooklyn, was quite different from that in the South. Brooklyn's black population suffered all the injustices of racism—de facto segregation, inadequate housing and education, and lack of police protection, social services, jobs, and decent food. They were also shut out of any access to political representation. However, they did not live like their southern brethren in an apartheid state of fear, violence, and death. In addition, the first wave of insurgent political leaders, whose major focus was to challenge the white racist structure of the Democratic Party in Brooklyn, consisted almost entirely of Caribbean immigrants and their children. Well educated in strict island British-model schools, they came to Brooklyn somewhat cosmopolitan, confident in their relationships with blacks as well as whites, and often looking askance at native-born African Americans. Like Chisholm, they or their parents had grown up on island colonies and never had the experience of being a racial minority or faced the stigma of American slavery and Jim Crow segregation. Even though many had lived under white colonial rule, they were accustomed to seeing blacks participating in a wider range of professions, even high political office.

Although voting and running black candidates for electoral office were important, many individuals and organizations believed that mass mobilizations of African Americans combined with nonviolent civil disobedience was a more effective way to force recalcitrant whites to listen to their grievances and enact meaningful civil rights legislation. In the 1950s, a time when Chisholm was somewhat politically active, the Brooklyn chapter of the NAACP expanded its established political role in order to tackle more explosive social issues facing central Brooklyn.

The most publicly confrontational and activist organization leading antiracist campaigns in Brooklyn was the local chapter of the Congress of Racial Equality. In the early 1960s, many people from Brooklyn went south with CORE to register voters or teach in the Freedom Schools, where volunteers taught black history and the philosophy of the civil rights movement. Brooklyn CORE was notable for initiating some of the more innovative actions against racial discrimination in housing, employment, and quality-of-life issues like garbage collection in predominantly black neighborhoods. Some people, like Thomas R. Jones, worked actively in the Democratic clubs as well as in CORE. As Brian Purnell demonstrates in his book about Brooklyn CORE, *Fighting Jim Crow in the County of Kings: The Congress of Racial Equality in Brooklyn,* Chisholm was not involved in CORE. No doubt, Chisholm believed that her political ambitions precluded radical extra electoral activity. She chose to work within and to reform the Democratic Party.

Brooklyn CORE organized successful campaigns for employment equality in the construction of Downstate Medical Center against employment discrimination, against housing discrimination, and for increasing the number of garbage pickups. Along with hundreds of other groups, Brooklyn CORE organized buses to bring thousands to the historic August 1963 March on Washington. But according to Donald Maggin, a Democratic Party activist who worked with Chisholm and other black Democrats and went to the march, Chisholm was not there.[1] Chisholm does not mention the March on Washington in her autobiography, and one can only speculate as to why she did not participate. Perhaps she was ill. Perhaps she was taking her annual summer vacation in the islands. Perhaps, as someone schooled in the anticolonial politics of the Caribbean, she did not identify with the southern civil rights movement. Or perhaps she did not think attending the march was necessary for her current or future political activism. After 1965, with Farmer's blessing, Brooklyn CORE began to move in the direction of Democratic Party politics.

Four years later, Farmer campaigned for Congress on the Republican ticket against Shirley Chisholm.

Chisholm's political consciousness was developing as a result of her political activism. She found the Black Muslims and the Nation of Islam intellectually exciting as a movement, particularly their leading spokesperson, Malcolm X. She had long discussions with her father about the ideas expounded by the Black Muslims. Malcolm X reminded Charles St. Hill of Marcus Garvey, especially his emphasis on achieving black pride and dignity without any help from whites. No doubt, St. Hill reveled in Malcolm's fearlessness in standing up to the white establishment. Malcolm X visited Brooklyn on a number of occasions, especially during Brooklyn CORE's campaign for job sharing at Downstate Medical Hospital. According to Maurice Fredericks, a CORE activist, Malcolm X was asked to join the picket line, which included African Americans, Puerto Ricans, and whites, but he refused, saying, "I'd be only too happy to walk with you just as soon as you get those devils off your line."[2] At that time, CORE was a racially integrated organization. Her admiration for Malcolm X's emphasis on black empowerment notwithstanding, Chisholm strongly opposed his ideas of black separatism and his disparagement of the March on Washington as the "Farce on Washington." No doubt she disagreed with his disparagement of Christianity and would have been appalled at the restrictive, subordinate roles allotted to women in the Nation of Islam.

Another political movement, feminism, which reemerged in the early 1960s, also had a great impact on Chisholm. In 1960 President Kennedy's Presidential Committee on the Status of Women, chaired by Eleanor Roosevelt, detailed massive discontent among women and underutilization of their talents. The 1963 publication of Betty Friedan's explosive feminist best-seller, *The Feminine Mystique*, coincided with the publication of the PCSW's report *The American Woman*. Both are credited with triggering the formation of the National Organization for Women, which represented one stream of the post-1945 women's movement. Chisholm joined NOW immediately after its founding.

Chisholm's reentry into Democratic Party politics began in 1960 when she joined with Thomas R. Jones and other veterans of the Flagg campaign to organize the Unity Democratic Club (UDC). Their goal was to overthrow the white Democratic Party machine. A serviceman who had risked his life during World War II, Jones was particularly determined to shake things up. Like many African American servicemen coming back from World War II, he had experienced Jim Crow, Brooklyn style, when he was refused entrance at Child's, a neighborhood restaurant on Nostrand Avenue. The owners "broke the glasses and threw them at my head," he remembered. " . . . I wasn't allowed to come in."

The Unity Democratic Club was somewhat remarkable for Brooklyn, or the rest of the country for that matter, in that women played leading roles. Ruth Goring was the Club's copresident. She had joined the UDC in order to address the issues of poverty and racism in her neighborhood as much as to elect black officials. The same could be said of Jocelyn Cooper, who hadn't thought much about politics, but was mainly concerned about making Bedford-Stuyvesant a better place to live. Jocelyn Cooper was married to Andrew Cooper, a lifelong Brooklyn resident and executive of the F. & M. Schaefer Brewing Company. Andrew Cooper left a permanent imprint on the state and national political landscape in the mid-1960s as lead plaintiff in a federal lawsuit that challenged the apportionment of congressional districts in Brooklyn. His lawsuit, *Cooper v. Power*, was one of a number of lawsuits challenging the nature of political representation. In 1962 and then in 1964, the Supreme Court ruled in *Baker v. Carr* and then *Reynolds v. Sims*, respectively, that reapportionment was constitutional. The impact of these court decisions cannot be underestimated, for reapportionment increased the political power of urban areas, and thus the Democratic Party. In Brooklyn *Cooper v. Power* resulted in the creation of New York's Twelfth Congressional District and, in 1968, the election of Shirley Chisholm to Congress.

The Unity Club was a reform organization and part of the Democratic Party's reform-minded Committee for Democratic Voters, which was composed of liberal whites. It was different from past clubs, for its members were largely well-educated, middle-class African Americans. It was racially integrated, and women held leadership positions. Goring, Cooper, and Chisholm, three leaders of the club, were determined to break with the politics of the old-boy networks, with their backroom deals and closed meetings. They insisted that the UDC be open and accessible to all. Chisholm understood that the UDC must first and foremost interest people in politics, educate them about the political process, and then get them to register to vote. Much of her understanding of the importance of educating voters no doubt came through her membership in the Brooklyn League of Women Voters, which was then a nonpartisan organization working to increase understanding of major public policy issues and to influence public policy through education and advocacy.

In this campaign Chisholm took to the streets and acquainted herself with people in her neighborhood and district, preparing her for her future electoral base. Canvassing with Cooper and Goring, she knocked on doors and rang doorbells in the district. Chisholm said that she "walked these streets until I almost went crazy." Jocelyn Cooper stressed the importance of door-to-door canvassing: "In order to get them, you've got to climb those stairs. . . . It doesn't work unless you are actually face-to-face. When they think you have an interest in asking them, they respond." Ruth Goring added, "We did an awful lot of political education on the role of politics in the life of the community, from the cradle to the grave. We were educating our own."[3] They all spent Saturday mornings in front of grocery stores, distributing information about voter registration. They recruited people to attend weekly meetings where the ABCs of local politics were taught: the names of their elected officials, who was a district leader, what was the role and purpose of a political club, what were the responsibilities of state legislators. The club ran aggressive voter registration drives, held programs to train election inspectors, called for changes in the law to allow registration by mail, and demanded that the attorney general send attorneys to monitor elections, in anticipation of voter intimidation and other problems facing voters on election day.

The fledgling UDC's platform was grounded in the day-to-day realities of African Americans' lives in Brooklyn. And their calls resonated with the larger national concerns. The UDC called for jobs and political access. As a way to demonstrate its commitment to the

Bedford-Stuyvesant community, the UDC joined Brooklyn CORE to publicly protest racial discrimination. When activists were arrested for disorderly conduct, the UDC's Tom Jones defended them. In 1960 the Unity Democratic Club joined with another reform club, the Nostrand Democratic Club, to run a more effective and racially integrated slate. This platform called for integration, better schools, higher wages, more jobs, better health care, housing and transportation, more street lighting, better sanitation, greater youth services for the neighborhood, and full representation and political access for African Americans and Puerto Ricans.

Once again, Chisholm found herself spending all her time working on the campaign, writing speeches, canvassing door to door, organizing rallies, speaking at rallies, phone banking, and fund-raising. In the past, she had vowed that she would never do this kind of grunt work again. But she never complained. The spirit of insurgency combined with the belief that now was the time to overthrow the white-controlled machine politics made all this work exciting and rewarding. To add to the political excitement and sense of purpose, the campaign was attracting national attention. Eleanor Roosevelt came to speak at a Jones-Rowe rally and drew four hundred people. Harry Belafonte, the legendary singer, actor, and activist, was the first on the UDC's list of endorsers. The campaign was exciting, but the insurgents were not successful the first time around. In the end, Berman and Carney defeated Jones and Rowe—though not by much. Jones lost 2,033 to 3,082. Carney lost by about the same margin. Both drew 42 percent of the vote.

Undaunted, they worked even harder for the next election. Shirley even convinced Conrad that they could win. He joined the UDC and worked alongside his wife, canvassing for voters. Liberal white reformers like the New York Committee for Democratic Voters endorsed the black-led insurgency. By 1962 the UDC had more members and was far better organized. It decided that it could run its own slate: Tom Jones for state assemblyman and Ruth Goring for district leader. The UDC ran an aggressive, confident campaign. "End Boss-ruled Plantation politics," read one leaflet. The UDC had struck a decisive blow against the white-dominated Democratic Party machine.

In the November election, Jones faced off against two African American women candidates, but in a city thoroughly dominated by the Democratic Party, Jones easily won. He and Ruth Goring were in charge of the district; the Unity Club was now *the* Democratic club in Brooklyn and for the first time controlled by African Americans.

Chisholm was elected to the Club Executive Committee, "just about back where I had started," she commented ironically. But there was a big difference, she noted. "This time I was one of the leaders of a group that was really representative of a district, and we were in a position, for the first time, to exert some leverage . . . on behalf of the people who had been second class citizens all their lives." There was still so much more to be done. In spite of the UDC's victory, there were only four African Americans on the twenty-two-member Democratic County Committee. Furthermore, racism and political cronyism continued to determine which political club received the spoils. The Democratic Party leadership used its clout to dilute the political power of the Unity Democrats. Jones complained, "The politicians who gave out the jobs . . . withheld from me the jobs and embellishments of office." Furthermore, the Unity Club was "starved out," he continued. "What they did was appoint my co-leader, Ruth Goring, to a job in the Borough President's office without telling me . . . so that she owed her job to them and not to me."[4] Chisholm was acutely aware of what was being done to the Unity Democrats, and, being ambitious and strategic, she began to understand that in order to get anything done in city politics, one had to find a way to straddle the old power structure while supporting the insurgents.

In 1964 Chisholm notified the Unity Democrats that she wanted the nomination for state representative to Albany. She was supremely confident that she had earned it. She had spent ten years doing every job in Brooklyn party politics, except running for elective office. She was equally convinced that she was the most qualified nominee, and she vowed, "I was not going to be denied because of my sex."[5] Now was the time to claim her destiny. She had the support and encouragement of her family. Her mother had always been behind her: "From the time I was two my mother said I was born to lead." Her father encouraged her political ambition, telling her, "If you work hard enough for what you want you'll get it." Conrad was equally positive: "It's what you want, Shirley, go out and get it."

Not all the men in the Unity Club shared her family's enthusiasm for her candidacy, and for the first time Chisholm experienced serious opposition from her male political comrades. She had to face down men in her own political club who "had a taste of how I operated," wrote Chisholm. To them she was "a little woman who didn't know how to play the game or when to shut up." The men in the club were reluctant to support Chisholm, not only because she appeared to be her own person, not bound to any one political club, but also because she had resolved that women should be nominated for elective office and given the same support as the men. Chisholm held her ground, believing herself the best candidate. Somewhat grudgingly, the UDC nominated her for the assembly seat.

Her nomination came at a time of great family tragedy. In the summer of 1963, Charles St. Hill came in from working in the garden, complaining of a bad headache. He sat down in his chair and died shortly thereafter of a general failure of his circulatory system. Chisholm was at work at the City Division of Day Care when she received the news. Screaming, she collapsed in grief. Not since the time she found out that her first fiancé was a criminal had she broken down so completely. Her father was one of the two most important people in her life. He had been her first political tutor, and as she grew up they became even closer, discussing the history, theory, strategy, and tactics of politics. In many respects, Charles was closer to Shirley than he was to his wife and three other daughters. Chisholm often thought the family dynamic pitted Shirley and Charles against her mother and her sisters. She wondered who could possibly fill the void. To compound the family heartbreak, before his death, Charles had set up a trust fund for Shirley with what was left of his savings. Only the house was left to Ruby, Odessa, Muriel, and Selma. Unfortunately, Charles's bequest created tremendous bitterness, and the rift in the St. Hill family never healed.

In spite of her grief, she went on with her campaign. Chisholm faced serious obstacles—obstacles every insurgent faces when preparing to challenge the incumbent. The first was money. She could not expect much help from the county organization, for it rarely gave as much to the black clubs as to the white clubs. The UDC did not have a big war chest, but it could provide dedicated volunteers, who now were doing all the campaign work that Chisholm had done in the past. But it cost money to pay for posters, leaflets, mailings, rent on meeting halls, and everything else needed to get out the vote. Conrad and Shirley went to their bank and took out four thousand dollars—a very large chunk from their savings.

Chisholm's greatest hurdle was the hostility she encountered because of her sex—hostility she would face for the rest of her political life. She was not the first African American woman from Brooklyn to campaign for state, city, or party office—Maude Richardson and Ada Jackson had run for office a decade earlier. Male chauvinism was so entrenched in all aspects of political life that Richardson's and Jackson's efforts did not smooth the path for the next generation of African American women. One day when Chisholm was out collecting nominating petitions, an elderly man who knew her and Conrad lit into her. "Young woman," he demanded of the forty-year-old Chisholm, "what are you doing out here in this cold? Did you get your husband's breakfast this morning? Did you straighten up your house? What are you doing running for office? This is something for men." Rather than get angry, Chisholm explained the ways in which she had served the Bedford-Stuyvesant community and that she was the best person to represent the district. The man wound up signing her electoral petition. The reason she never struck back at her male hecklers, Chisholm wrote, was that she "understood too well their reasons for lashing out at black women; in a society that denied them real manhood, I was threatening their shaky self-esteem even more."[6] Once again, these local elections schooled her for later challenges. Throughout her political career, especially when she ran for the US presidency in 1972, she would always have to face men who tried to infantilize, patronize, or demonize her.

With the skills she had learned in the political clubhouses and in community organizations, she knew how to play up her strengths as an African American and as a woman. She also knew when to attack the party machine, and when to support it. Instead of reacting to the gendered criticisms, she used them to her advantage. Always a meticulous planner, she knew that there were five thousand more women than men registered to vote in the Seventeenth Assembly District. She appealed directly to these women, urging them to "elect me to dramatize the problems of black women." She also called upon Brooklyn clubwomen for help. Chisholm had served as the Brooklyn branch president of Key Women of America, a civic organization committed to the protection of children, family services, and community needs. Key Women of America was an organization in the tradition of black women's clubs, which focused on respect and uplift. Constance Rose, one of Key Women's officers, said, "We all got in and pitched for her. . . . We were actually her backbone."[7] Years before the concept "gender gap" was coined, Chisholm discovered how it could work to her advantage in Bedford-Stuyvesant. Her campaign took place during the first stirrings of the women's movement. At this time, Chisholm did not identify herself as a women's rights activist, but she was involved in and a member of many Brooklyn women's organizations—church, community, political, and social. Furthermore, she knew from experience that Brooklyn women were the backbone of all Brooklyn's political organizations. This first campaign assuredly planted the seeds of her later feminism.

She won the election handily, first beating her Democratic Party primary opponent, Harold Brady, 4,290 to 1,729. In the general election, she sailed to victory with 18,151 votes to the Republican Charles Lewis's 1,893. Simon Golar, the Liberal candidate, received only 922 votes. The Key Women celebrated Chisholm's victory. The headline in their newsletter rejoiced, "We salute a Lady of Color. . . . This is a year for dreams to come true. Dr. Martin Luther King receives the Nobel Peace prize and Shirley becomes our representative in Albany, New York."[8] The Unity Democratic Club hosted a joyous victory celebration. Chisholm was not the first black woman elected to state office—Bessie Buchanan from Harlem had been elected to the assembly a decade earlier—but this time not being first did not bother her. At last she had been elected to office; at last she had some power to make changes for her community. She had a power base largely made up of women in her district; she was developing as a speaker and a political strategist. Perhaps now she would be treated with the respect she had earned.

5

New York State Assemblywoman

Shirley Chisholm took the oath of office as a New York State assemblywoman in January 1965. Before her election, she had traveled to the state capital, Albany, three times, leading delegations to lobby legislators. Now she was there to represent the needs of her constituents—the poor, the elderly, the young, women, African Americans, and Latinos—those who had previously been marginalized and ignored.

Chisholm was part of the liberal landslide that elected Robert F. Kennedy to the US Senate from New York and Lyndon Johnson as president. She was sworn in with the largest Democratic majority since 1939 and alongside the largest number of black legislators in New York State's history. In the four years Chisholm served as assemblywoman, the number of African American and Latino legislators increased, but only by a few. During her tenure as a legislator, she worked closely with four extraordinary African American political actors: Percy Sutton, later the Manhattan Borough president; David Dinkins, later the first African American mayor of New York City; Charles Rangel, elected to the House of Representatives in 1971; and Basil Paterson, later deputy mayor under Ed Koch and New York secretary of state. Better known as the "Gang of Four," they made up the black Democratic Party political leadership of Manhattan, situated in Harlem, which continued to be the heart and soul of black America. Called the Harlem Clubhouse, these men have dominated Harlem politics since 1960 and have become national spokespersons for black political activism.

The New York State Legislature was notorious as one of the more dysfunctional state legislatures. No sooner had Chisholm been sworn in than the majority Democratic Party began, in Chisholm's words, "an historic and ridiculous two month fight" over who would be the next Speaker of the House. Chisholm was drawn into this fight immediately because the two contenders, Stanley Steingut and Anthony Travia, were both from Brooklyn. Each man believed that he was the logical heir, Steingut because his father had been House Speaker and Travia because he had been the minority leader during the years of Republican control. The fight immobilized the entire legislature for two months, since the state senate could not enact any legislation without the assembly, and the assembly could not act until the leadership question was resolved. The Democrats engaged in countless huddles, meetings, and caucuses, running from the state capitol to the various hotel suites in the nearby DeWitt Clinton hotel where they caucused, huddled, and met some more. Chisholm watched her colleagues' machinations with exasperation and displeasure. She was also unhappy that no one was paying attention to her. She was not invited to caucus meetings, and no one asked why she did not go into Steingut's suite, as all his other supporters did. She understood that she was a newcomer to Albany and was expected to listen, learn, and vote as she was told to. But she also knew that she was invisible because of her gender, and that rankled her.

Rather than nurse a grudge or complain, though, Chisholm turned this slight to her advantage, a tactic she had learned in her assembly campaign. Understanding that she could not do anything legislatively while the Democrats were bickering, she decided to prove to all that she would be her own person—independent of even her own clubhouse, thus setting the stage for her later campaign slogan, "Unbought and Unbossed." A Brooklyn political leader named Howard Shakin, a former classmate of Chisholm's at Brooklyn College, assumed she would vote for Steingut, pointing out that "it's good to be on the winning side." "Who told you I was going to vote for Stanley?" Chisholm replied. Dumbfounded, Shakin replied that everyone was expecting her to vote for Steingut. "Everybody but me," she retorted. "[A]ll of you have a nerve assuming where my vote will go." Then she announced, "I'm casting my vote for Anthony Travia."[1] Even though she was warned that not going along with the Democratic clubs would be committing political suicide, she and another Brooklyn assemblyperson, Bertram Baker, voted for Travia. She even broke tradition as a new legislator by making a speech on the floor of the assembly supporting Travia. It turned out that her vote did not matter. At the last minute, the entire Republican caucus in the assembly voted for Travia, giving him the speakership.

Chisholm's decision to defy her own Brooklyn club leadership was not made in a fit of pique. Rather, her action represented careful political positioning, something she did over again once elected to Congress in 1968. She was very aware of the challenges facing someone who was black, female, and a brand-new legislator. Much of the initial hostility she faced was a reaction to her being such an outspoken black woman—something the clubmen did not appreciate. Steingut, for example, had worked with Chisholm in Brooklyn politics for more than a decade. He observed that although he thought Chisholm was "nice" and "bright," she did not play by his rules. But she had not come to Albany to go along with "the rules of the political game," which she observed were "designed to make it possible for men in power to control the actions of their supporters and stay there." Having spent twenty years in the trenches of Brooklyn club politics, she wanted to shake things up. "If I wasn't a maverick in the political power brokers' books before the Travia-Steingut face-off, I was from then on."[2] This initial confrontation with the party machine seemed to work for her. She established her reputation for being her own person and for having the courage of her independent convictions. The confidence she gained from this first struggle would continue throughout her political career.

During the two-month leadership battle, Chisholm spent more time in Brooklyn than in Albany. But once the speakership issue was settled, she spent a good five days each week in the capital. She would take the train or bus up early Monday morning and return home on weekends. Her days were filled with committee meetings and legislative sessions. Her nights were spent in her room at the DeWitt Clinton hotel across the street from the capitol building, where she pored over pending legislation, prepared herself for the next day's committee work, watched some television, and read. No doubt, her evenings were lonely. Albany at that time was not particularly welcoming to African Americans, and in the mid 1960s "respectable" women did not go out to restaurants or bars on their own. Once the day's legislative session ended, the male legislators would go off to bars, movies, restaurants, and clubs. Not a single one of Chisholm's colleagues ever invited her to their social gatherings. When asked about this, Albert Blumenthal, assemblyman from Manhattan's Sixty-Ninth District, admitted that he could not recall anyone in his crowd ever inviting Chisholm to join them, and he could not say why. "My impression of Shirley," Blumenthal surmised, for he never asked Chisholm herself, was "that she preferred to take her work back to the hotel with her at night." Chisholm herself told an interviewer, "I don't blame the fellows for not asking me out to dinner. I think there was a little fear of 'how do we handle her socially?'" She added that "men don't like independent women. Not many knew I was a regular gal. I think they were afraid to take the chance." Chisholm, who loved to go out to dinner and movies and especially to go dancing, would have liked to be invited to some of the social events. She covered up her disappointment by remarking, "I do not care for the night life of the New York State legislature."[3]

This solitary lifestyle must have been more difficult than Chisholm let on. She was away from her husband. She had just lost her beloved father, and she was estranged from her mother and sisters. She was also far away from her church, the women of the Key Club, and the many other community, political, and social organizations that sustained her in Brooklyn. She never complained, preferring to focus on being a successful legislator, and once the state's business began in earnest, she was in her element. She found herself in awe of the assembly chamber with its rows of green leather chairs and polished desks—the place where bills were drafted, legislators speechified, and votes were taken. She loved the spirit of partisan combat.

After all, she had been a champion debater at Brooklyn College, and now she could put her debating skills to the test. Albert Blumenthal, who was also the deputy minority leader, remembered Chisholm as a "very tough lady, likable but a loner. Unlike other women in the legislature, she was never afraid to jump into a debate." Describing her as someone "who knew what she wanted and said it well," he ended with a backhanded compliment. "Enemies like Shirley," he said half humorously, "nobody needs in politics."[4]

Chisholm worked closely with Charles Rangel and David Dinkins, but she was closest to Percy Sutton. She was very proud when "the Associated Press called us the two most militant and effective black members of the Assembly."[5] In her four years as an assemblywoman, she was a remarkably active legislator, introducing fifty bills, eight of which passed. This is an impressive record, considering how many bills get introduced and how few even reach the floor of the assembly chamber. As a member of the Committee on Education, she crafted many of the bills that came out of that committee. Her legislation reflected her political social justice outlook and the needs of her Brooklyn constituents, as well as the spirit of progressive liberalism that was at its peak from 1964 to 1968.

This period of great progressive reform was a result of the mass movement for civil rights. The demand for an end to racial segregation and for equal political access led to a heightened sense of social citizenship. Millions of people of color, the poor, aged, women, and those involved in agriculture, domestic, and service industries were demanding that the New Deal social programs and legislative reforms of the 1930s and '40s, which had for the most part benefited only white urban males, be expanded to include all Americans. The 1964 Democratic landslide, which won the presidency as well as majority control in both houses of Congress, gave rise to a new post–New Deal vision of liberalism that called for new ways to achieve greater economic social justice and equality. The "Great Society," as President Lyndon Johnson termed it, was based on the belief that massive government funding would speed up economic growth, which would then enable the government to provide public funding for welfare, housing, health, and educational programs.

The Great Society's liberal vision and legislative record changed the economic, political, and social landscape of the United States, as Congress passed a series of programs, including civil rights, an end to segregation, Medicare and Medicaid, extension of welfare, immigration reform, federal aid to education at all levels, subsidies for the arts and humanities, environmental activism, and a series of programs designed to wipe out poverty. The War on Poverty programs motivated the creation of new agencies and encouraged community participation, resulting in new forms of community activism, such as the National Welfare Rights Organization, domestic-rights workers' groups, and local educational reform associations. Chisholm was politically attuned to the policies of the Great Society, and she supported the many community groups created in its wake.

Her first successful piece of legislation, of which she was very proud, was a bill that set up New York State's first unemployment insurance coverage for personal and domestic employees. Every employer who paid a domestic five hundred dollars or more a year had to make contributions to their unemployment insurance. Until Chisholm introduced this legislation, domestic workers could not count on a steady income, and if an employer went on vacation or just terminated their services, they could not count on any form of unemployment insurance. Speaking about the need for such legislation, Chisholm movingly recounted the difficulties her own mother faced when, through no fault of her own, she lost her job and could not bring in needed income for the family.

With this legislation, she achieved a major goal that the civil rights and labor movements had advocated for almost three decades. Roosevelt had excluded domestic workers from unemployment insurance as part of a bargain with racist southern Democratic Party politicians, to win their support for New Deal legislation. Forty-five years after Chisholm's bill was passed, in 2010, New York State's domestic workers finally won a Domestic Workers' Bill of Rights, giving them the right to overtime pay, days of rest, protection under the New York State Human Rights Law, and the creation of a special cause of action for those who suffered sexual or racial harassment. Chisholm's legislation paved the way for this progressive law.

Another bill, of which she was also proud, reflected her lifelong commitment to access to higher education: the introduction of SEEK (Search for Education, Elevation, and Knowledge). This program sought out African American and Latino high school students (at the time, most Latinos were Puerto Rican) to give them state scholarships so they could attend the colleges in either the CUNY (City University of New York) or the SUNY (State University of New York) system. In 1965, when Chisholm entered the state legislature, CUNY, led by Chancellor Albert Bowker, was being transformed from a collection of independent four-year and two-year community colleges, including Brooklyn College, to a more centralized twenty-campus university. Of its 100,000 students, less than 2 percent were students of color. Chancellor Bowker approached Julius C. C. Edelstein, then an Albany lobbyist for CUNY, asking for his assistance in developing programs that would enable students of color to successfully attend institutions of higher education. Edelstein approached Chisholm, who chaired the legislative Committee on Education. She was totally supportive of the proposed SEEK program; making its passage a top priority, she worked alongside Basil Paterson, David Dinkins, and Percy Sutton to win financing and draft legislation for the program. SEEK was not just a financial program but also an educational assistance program. Recognizing that students in underfunded urban schools did not receive the same educational opportunities as students in the more affluent suburbs or in private schools, SEEK provided students with extra tutoring and counseling. In its first two years of operation, more than 8,000 students received scholarships. CUNY's enrollment jumped from fewer than 100,000 students to more than 250,000. Today, as a result of Chisholm, Sutton, Dinkins, and Paterson's legislative achievements, the student body at both SUNY and CUNY reflects the enormous diversity of the New York metropolitan area, and SEEK programs are an integral component of the academic life of these institutions. Chisholm always hoped to create national legislation that would create SEEK programs to benefit all college and university students.

Chisholm's other pieces of legislation reflected her commitment to her constituents. For example, she proposed bills that especially benefited women, such as day-care centers for the children of working parents or families receiving public assistance. She was responsible for the passage of successful legislation that protected seniority for teachers who took maternity leaves, thus giving pregnant teachers job security. She introduced a bill to raise the amount of money local schools spent per pupil, of which the state would pay a share. She achieved a major goal that the civil rights and labor movement had advocated for almost three decades. She won passage of a bill that extended unemployment insurance and Social Security protections to agricultural and domestic workers.

Finally, Chisholm positioned herself with the emerging women's movement in two major campaigns. In 1967, as a vice president of the New York City chapter of the National Organization for Women, she headed the NOW-NYC campaign at the state constitutional convention for legislation to guarantee women's equal rights. She also used her position as a state legislator to move forward legislation to legalize abortion. She signed her name to press releases and public letters on NOW-NYC stationery that called upon the state legislators to consider that "the right to terminate a pregnancy shall be deemed a civil right." Three years later, and as a result of much public agitation from the radical women's liberation movement, the legislature passed a law expanding abortion rights and eliminating restrictions on the practice of abortion. Of the 207 legislators, just 4 were women.

Not all Chisholm's proposed bills were successful. For example, she introduced legislation prohibiting discrimination in banking, investment, and insurance practices. She fought for unemployment insurance for hospital workers as well as for a minimum-wage law. She was particularly disappointed when legislation she vehemently opposed, granting state money to church-run schools, passed 136–8. She felt equally let down when a bill mandating every police officer in New York State complete courses in civil rights, civil liberties, and race relations failed.

In spite of these defeats and her occasional loneliness in Albany, Chisholm emerged from her experience in the assembly even more confident and self-assured. Her political mettle was strengthened by having to run for reelection twice more, in 1965 and 1966, due to constant redistricting. At first she was furious, believing that the party leaders were trying to harass her. Each time she had to wage two campaigns—a primary fight and another in the regular election—which meant raising money, organizing volunteers, and campaigning. But this was the system, and she won the primaries and the general elections handily. "I proved to be the top vote-getter," she said. "I always pulled higher than the top of the ticket."[6]

After four years in the state legislature, Chisholm reflected that she had received an advanced degree in district and county politics. She did not like most of what she saw and learned. For one thing, she was constantly frustrated by the male chauvinism of her colleagues. "This whole question of women, it gets to you," she remarked in an interview. "You can use women to do all sorts of tasks, but to put a woman in power, well that's another thing."[7] The consistent support from her husband, as well as from the women of the Bedford-Stuyvesant community, no doubt was a source of strength. Thus, her emerging feminism was forged in the halls of the Albany state legislature, in her political club meetings, and with the women in her constituency.

She was further disappointed by the behavior of many of her colleagues—Republicans as well as Democrats. She felt that they saw their time in the state legislature more as a time to party than to conduct serious business. She was very concerned about the corrupting power of party bosses and political lobbyists, for she witnessed how legislators could be forced to vote against their conscience or against the best interests of their constituents after just one phone call. Those in power threatened independent legislators by denying them desired committee positions, organizing primary opposition, and isolating them from their colleagues. Chisholm was aware of the political price she would pay for her insistence on independence, and she was willing to suffer the consequences. At the same time, she knew that to be an effective politician who could navigate legislation through the state assembly, she had to work with party leaders and bosses. In fact, she believed she had been an effective legislator, as well as an independent people's advocate. "I have guts," she would state proudly, and affirmed that she was determined "to belong to no one but the people."[8]

Chisholm's tenure in the legislature convinced her that she had the talent, the ability, and the passion to represent her constituents. Although she was not the first black woman to serve in Albany, she believed she was the first to make a meaningful contribution. The men in Bedford-Stuyvesant who had earlier told her to go back to the kitchen had come to respect her. The women of her district were steadfast supporters. Her constituents knew that Chisholm would be their fiercest defender. Through hard work, grit, determination, and almost unbelievable self-confidence, Shirley Chisholm had built a power base in central Brooklyn, and she intended to use it. The lessons she learned in Albany prepared her for her next undertaking: Washington.

6

I Am Woman

The year 1968—when Shirley Chisholm became the first African American woman elected to the US Congress—was a watershed year, a tumultuous year, as well as a year full of contradictions. Chisholm's election as the first "black woman congressman," as she preferred to call herself, catapulted her to the front pages of the nation's newspapers. Yet this was only one of the many extraordinary events of that cataclysmic year.

Chisholm's election took place against a background of massive global, national, and local turmoil, discontent, protest, violence—and at the same time a sense of hope. There were worldwide demonstrations against the US war in Vietnam, and the United States itself was bitterly divided over foreign policy. Young people rose up in protest in Australia, Brazil, Czechoslovakia, England, France, Germany, Japan, Mexico, Poland, and the United States, challenging the global economic, political, social, and cultural order. The US civil rights movement inspired political activism by oppressed minorities in Northern Ireland and South Africa.

The southern civil rights movement was being transformed. One wing, led by Martin Luther King Jr., believed the black movement should oppose the war in Vietnam as well as wage an integrated struggle for economic and social justice and continue to work within the Democratic Party. Another wing, collectively described as the Black Power movement, was more left leaning and militant, advocating more confrontational positions such as open hostility to whites, black-only organizations, armed self-defense of the black community as well as support for communist countries such as Cuba and China. In April King was assassinated, and a number of cities, including Washington, Baltimore, Louisville, Kansas City, and Seattle, erupted in flames, signaling a bitter end to the once hopeful, nonviolent, integrated civil rights movement.

A month and a half later, Senator Robert Kennedy, brother of murdered president John F. Kennedy, was shot and killed in a Los Angeles hotel kitchen after winning the California presidential primary. The two leading voices of moderate opposition to US Cold War politics and support for greater racial and economic justice were now silenced.

Young people were in open revolt against their parents and opposed to what they described as the "establishment." Throwing off the restrictive mores of the 1950s, many experimented with drugs, sex, and unconventional lifestyles. Others, mainly college students, demonstrated against the war in Vietnam, walked picket lines in support of striking farmworkers, demonstrated against racism, and organized sit-ins on their college campuses, demanding greater participation in the life of the academy.

Radicalized and outraged by the continuing war in Vietnam, the escalation of racist violence, and the refusal or inability of the nation's leaders to listen to their anger, thousands converged on Chicago in August 1968 to make their voices heard at the Democratic Party National Convention. Liberal delegates to the convention, including Chisholm, were furious that party rules unfairly silenced dissent, so that the antiwar sentiment had no voice. Thousands protested in the streets outside the convention hall against the war and Mayor Richard Daley's police brutality. Violence and chaos ensued, resulting in ever-greater bitterness within the Democratic Party.

Women's enormous discontent and dissatisfaction with the American dream, as documented by the President's Commission on the Status of Women, had been gathering steam for some time. In 1963 Betty Friedan's *Feminine Mystique* made it to the best-seller's list. In 1966 the National Organization for Women, led by Friedan, was organized, and Chisholm was a member. However, the media as well as the majority of elected officials remained unconcerned with issues of gender. Then in September 1968, members of a group called New York Radical Women staged a protest of the "American-as-apple-pie" Miss America Contest in Atlantic City.[1] This protest brought to center stage the emergence of the women's liberation movement, which, of all the liberation movements that erupted in the sixties, left the most lasting imprint on the world and was arguably the largest of all the social protest movements that emerged in the late 1950s and '60s. Almost all the protesters were veterans of the civil rights and antiwar movements, but in Atlantic City they were demonstrating against the use of women as sex objects to sell racism, militarism, and mindless consumerism. The Miss America protest brought the issues of gender and pervasive sex discrimination to the front pages of the newspapers and unleashed millions of women to fight for equality. The more radical women's liberation movement embraced Chisholm. Shirley Chisholm, a member of NOW and an outspoken feminist, supported many of the actions and demands of the younger women, but did not participate in most of their events.

The continuing opposition to the war in Vietnam as well as the escalating Black Power protests in 1968 ended Lyndon Johnson's presidency and fractured the old New Deal Democratic Party Coalition. This tumultuous year marked the beginning of the end of post–World War II liberalism, despite the massive movements for greater social justice, equality, and peace. The gains of the civil rights movement—in particular the enfranchisement of African Americans in the South—transformed both the Republican and the Democratic Parties. In his successful presidential campaign, the anticommunist Cold Warrior Richard Nixon denounced urban unrest and many of Johnson's Great Society programs, directing his appeal to southern whites and disaffected northern ethnic workers. For the first time since the 1860s, the white South went Republican. African Americans, Latinos, and others involved in social protest movements in large numbers joined the Democratic Party.

Tumultuous changes were taking place in Brooklyn as well. There were student walkouts and sit-ins at Brooklyn colleges and schools, protests against the war in Vietnam, and demonstrations against racism, police brutality, and the assassination of King. But the most polarizing event, which divided Brooklyn and the rest of the city, was a months-long public schoolteachers' strike, in which every Brooklyn politician and political activist from the neighborhoods of Ocean Hill–Brownsville and Bedford-Stuyvesant, including Shirley Chisholm, had to take a side. This bitterly fought confrontation involved the recently created community-controlled school board in the largely black Ocean Hill–Brownsville section of Brooklyn and New York City's teachers' union, the United Federation of Teachers (UFT). Community control of public schools was a new phenomenon in a city where, in 1968, the school system was one of the most racially segregated in the United States, with the whitest professional staff in the country. Ninety percent of the teachers and all but two of the principals were white. A majority of the Brooklyn teachers were Jewish, which led to accusations of anti-Semitism. The strike was triggered by the school board's transfer of twelve white teachers and seven white assistant principals out of the district. It dragged on from May 1968 to November 1968, shutting down the public schools for a total of thirty-six days. Racial and political tensions between blacks and whites, between the UFT and the Ocean Hill–Brownsville community, and between teachers who went out on strike and those (70 percent of them white) who crossed the picket lines to teach reached the boiling point on many occasions. The UFT leadership charged the community with anti-Semitism. The community accused the striking teachers of racism.

The strike ended with an apparent victory for the teachers: the seventy-nine teachers who had been transferred or had walked out in sympathy were reinstated, and an agreement was worked out that reaffirmed due process rights for New York City educators. Chisholm was peripherally involved in the strike. She supported Ocean Hill–Brownsville's community control of the schools and said so as she campaigned for political office. But during the early months of the strikes, she had been hospitalized and could not attend many of the meetings. In addition, Ocean Hill–Brownsville was not part of her electoral district, so she did not spend time campaigning there. If anything during this strike, Chisholm learned as a campaigner how to effectively straddle polarizing political positions. Chisholm was attacked by both sides of the dispute: some Brooklyn College alums from the sixties and Albert Shanker, president of the striking teachers' union, attacked her for supporting the alleged anti-Semitism of the community activist. Jitu Weusi, a central figure defending the Ocean Hill–Brownsville community control, was very critical of what he described as Chisholm's lukewarm support.[2] The aftermath was bitterness within the UFT; a growing rift within the civil rights, African American, and Jewish communities; more white flight out of central Brooklyn; continued deterioration of central Brooklyn's schools; and an increasing racial divide in the borough. This split between the Jewish and African American communities, brought to the fore during the strike, only continued to grow.

Critical congressional elections took place during this year of unrest. Redistricting changes that had begun in 1964 set the stage for a new Twelfth Congressional District, which would for the first time give Brooklyn's African Americans the opportunity to elect one of their own. The new district was centered in Bedford-Stuyvesant, Chisholm's neighborhood, and included sections of three other neighborhoods: Williamsburg, Crown Heights, and Bushwick. Demographically, the district was 70 percent black and Puerto Rican and 30 percent white, and 80 percent of its voters were registered Democrats. In anticipation of the election of an African American to Congress, and even before the district's boundaries had been settled, an ad hoc group, the Citizens' Committee for a Negro Congressman, was formed to vet potential Democratic candidates.

Once the new congressional district became a reality, Chisholm, who inexplicably had not demonstrated support for the voting-rights lawsuit when Cooper introduced it in 1966, began planning and plotting her congressional campaign. "Before I make a move, I analyze everything," she explained in an interview, and indeed she was acutely aware of the obstacles she faced. First and foremost was her gender. All the party leaders in her district were men who had shown a distinct dislike of female candidates. The black party leaders were even more disposed than the white ones to support a man, a common sentiment at the time, for they had intense feelings about solidifying the image of the strong black male. The second obstacle she faced was her independence. Although the Brooklyn Unity Club would support her, the Brooklyn County organization might not, knowing that they could not control her. She and Conrad pored over the election rolls and census statistics to better understand the new district. She already knew that the majority was black, but she learned that Italians lived in Bushwick, Jews in Crown Heights, and Puerto Ricans in Williamsburg. Even before she decided to run, she lived for a while in a Bushwick housing project, in order to get to know the women. One demographic became particularly important to Chisholm: there were thousands more female registered voters than male. She estimated that there were somewhere between ten and thirty thousand more women and determined that if she ran, she would make her appeal to them.

One event convinced the Chisholms that she should run and she could win. On a cold February evening, an elderly woman knocked on their door and handed her an envelope, saying that a group of women had collected money for her congressional campaign. Chisholm opened the envelope and found $9.62, all in coins. Overcome with emotion, with tears streaming down her cheeks, Chisholm promised this woman, "I know what this money means to you. We'll make it together—you and I." Later that night, she told Conrad that she would always treasure this envelope. "That woman has probably spent her whole life as a domestic. She could have been my own mother." She understood that "women like that are worth more to me than the opinions of a thousand politicians."[3]

By January 1968, the speculation and gossip over who would announce their intention to run for Congress were intense. The black legislators in Albany could talk about nothing else. Who would the Democrats choose? The Republicans? Wishing to jump-start her campaign before the others joined in, Chisholm was the first to announce her candidacy. All in all, twelve people announced their intention to run. Chisholm was the only woman, and this gender imbalance worked to her advantage. Women in the New York State Democratic Party were pushing for more women in Congress. Bernice Brown from Brooklyn explained that the women's Democratic Party caucus was "making sure that we got some females in there because everything was male. . . . Shirley Chisholm was the best we had."[4] Chisholm, along with the other candidates, met with the Citizens Committee, and even though their vote carried no political weight in the Democratic Party, Chisholm was their unanimous choice. Although she was surprised at this support, she was confident it was based upon three factors: she had the nerve and courage to disagree with the Democratic Party leadership when she felt she had to, she had the confidence and poise to win over the electorate, and, finally, she had won three elections for state assembly.

Not surprisingly, the county leadership, all men, which had initially promised not to get involved in the candidate selection process, began fielding its own candidates for a primary battle. They had always distrusted Chisholm for her refusal to accept strict party discipline. "If we can't control her in Albany," they complained, "how are we going to in Washington?"[5] The county organization favored William C. Thompson, former state senator, who was rumored to have the tacit support of Robert F. Kennedy, then a US senator from New York, and Stanley Steingut, two men with considerable clout with white district leaders. Chisholm was not particularly impressed with their influence. "Willie felt the white boys were going to get out the vote for him," she remarked dismissively. The leadership's other candidate was a local political clubwoman, Dolly Robinson, who had run unsuccessfully for various political offices.

The year 1968 was also a presidential election year, and Hubert Humphrey, Eugene McCarthy, and Robert Kennedy were running for the Democratic Party nomination. Each Brooklyn hopeful supported a different presidential aspirant: Dolly Robinson ran as a Humphrey candidate, Thompson as a Kennedy candidate, and Chisholm, miffed at Robert Kennedy's refusal to support her candidacy, was sympathetic to Eugene McCarthy. After Kennedy's assassination, Chisholm regretted her feelings of resentment and severed her ties with the McCarthy campaign.

Chisholm was preparing for a grueling three-way primary when out of the blue, her former mentor, Wesley McDonald Holder, called her and after ten years of political enmity offered his support and organizational skills. Holder, who had said he wanted to live long enough to elect a black judge and a black congressperson, was now in his seventies and saw his chance with Chisholm. "You can't win without me and people in the streets," he said, assuring her. "You're the easiest product to sell and I am going to organize the campaign and sell you." Bygones had become bygones, and the two renewed their political partnership. Mac also understood the implications of the census reports and polling data. Even though the new congressional district was 70 percent black and Puerto Rican, he told Chisholm not only would she have to win the majority of the black vote, but the white vote would be crucial for her to prevail in a three-way race. She also enlisted the backing of Julius C. C. Edelstein, who had worked with her in Albany and remembered her support for the SEEK program. He became her financial adviser. Longtime Brooklyn pol Thomas Fortune managed her campaign.

Chisholm and Holder worked nineteen hours a day. Mac used his organizational skills and political connections to arrange meetings and speaking engagements and to raise money. They both knew that to win, she had to go out into the neighborhoods where she was not that well known, and she did. Instead of relying on mailings, Chisholm took to the streets of Williamsburg, Crown Heights, Bushwick, and Bedford-Stuyvesant, asking everyone for support. She campaigned on street corners, in the parks, and in the housing projects. She campaigned from a sound truck, holding a bullhorn and saying "Ladies and Gentleman, this is Fighting Shirley Chisholm coming through." Her supporters would then distribute thousands of flyers as Chisholm answered questions and explained her political point of view. "I have a theory about campaigning," she said. "You have to let them feel you."[6]

Chisholm decided that she needed a slogan. Capitalizing on her well-crafted persona as a political renegade—"I'm not connected to the big boys, "she often said—she came up with "Fighting Shirley Chisholm: Unbought and Unbossed."[7] She had the phrase *Unbought and Unbossed* printed on shopping bags, bumper stickers, posters, and flyers that were distributed everywhere. On the weekends, she traveled with a caravan of twenty cars driven by supporters. Each car bore a picture of Chisholm with the slogan "Vote for Shirley Chisholm for Congress—Unbought and Unbossed."

In her autobiography, Chisholm wrote that her slogan "said it all." And it did. She claimed that it demonstrated to her community that she was fiercely independent; she could never be the pawn of the party pols. Basil Paterson agreed that the slogan "signified not just her pride in herself, but almost an arrogance, a wonderful defiant arrogance that she had in her, that once she started speaking, she didn't care who you were; she was calling it like she saw it. She was so good at it."[8] The slogan signified more than just opposition to the machine and party bosses. As historian Josh Guild explained, it signified "racial and gender liberation." *Unbought* meant more than just that her vote was not for sale. It referred to liberation from slavery and colonialism. In the same vein, *unbossed* signified not only that she was not going to be dominated by any one political organization, but also that she was a strong woman, not to be bossed around at work, within political organizations, or at home.[9] Her slogan stayed with her throughout her political career and became the title of her autobiography.

Chisholm made a point of involving women in her campaign. "Make no bones about it," she said over and over again at women's meetings. "You will send me to Congress."[10] She contacted every neighborhood woman leader and asked for help. They held raffles, teas, bake sales, and barbecues. "In the black neighborhoods I ate chitlins, in the Jewish neighborhoods bagels and lox, in the Puerto Rican neighborhoods arroz con pollo," she wrote.[11] Chisholm knew that these women were transforming the traditional meaning of "woman's work": working for a man. This time the women were doing the same work, but for a woman. "If they were successful," she said, "they would have helped elect the first black woman ever to serve in the House of Representatives."

In this primary race, Chisholm was the underdog. Thompson was so convinced he would win that he took a vacation on Cape Cod in the middle of the campaign. On primary day, Chisholm nervously watched the returns from the black districts. Voter turnout was very low. Perhaps the promise of the first African American representative from Brooklyn was not enough to bring voters to the polls. Nevertheless, Chisholm astounded the pundits and won the primary. Of the 12,000 votes cast, she beat Thompson, who received 4,907 votes, by about 1,000. Dolly Robinson, who came in third, took votes away from Thompson, not Chisholm. Chisholm carried all four white sections in the district.

She had little time to savor her victory. In Brooklyn, a heavily Democratic borough, winning the Democratic primary usually meant an easy electoral victory in the fall. Not in this tumultuous year. Sensing political opportunities in the newly created Twelfth District, the New York State Republican Party, which was far more liberal than the national Republican Party, approached James Farmer, who had resigned his position as the head of CORE. Earlier, the New York State Republican Party had considered asking Farmer to fill the Senate seat made vacant by Robert Kennedy's assassination. Nothing came of this, so the New York State Republican Party asked him to run for Congress in the Twelfth District. The New York Republicans and Farmer were confident that because of Farmer's stature as a courageous civil rights leader, he could win the support of Brooklyn's African American voters, even though they were registered and voted overwhelmingly Democratic. Farmer did not mind running on the Republican ticket, but knowing how much the black community disliked Nixon he accepted with the caveat that he would never do anything to support the election of Richard Nixon. His first action as a candidate was to call a press conference announcing that he was endorsing Hubert Humphrey for president.

When Chisholm heard that Farmer was going to be running on both the Republican and the Liberal tickets, she exploded, "He doesn't even live in Brooklyn!" "Why doesn't he run for something in Harlem?" she asked Mac Holder. He explained that there were no residency laws for running for Congress, and besides Farmer rented an apartment in Bedford-Stuyvesant "for appearances' sake." Chisholm and Holder knew that this "carpetbagger," as Chisholm sneeringly called Farmer, would be a formidable opponent.

To make matters worse, in July she became seriously ill with a massive fibroid tumor. Chisholm did not mind the stay at the hospital as much as she chafed at her lengthy convalescence. Even though she was a delegate to the 1968 Democratic Party convention and was elected to the post of national committee member from New York State, she had to sit through the convention in bed in a nearby hotel. By the time she returned to Brooklyn, she was eager to get back into the campaign. Farmer, who had been campaigning all this time, began to taunt her: "Where's Mrs. Chisholm? We haven't seen or heard from her." Determined to get back on the campaign trail, she called her doctor and said, "Look, the stitches aren't in my mouth. I'm going out." Wrapping a beach towel around her hips, to hide all the weight she had lost, she walked down the three flights of her house, grabbed a bullhorn, and walked up and down the streets calling out, declaring, "Ladies and gentlemen, this is fighting Shirley Chisholm and I am up and around in spite of what people are saying."[12]

At first sight, Farmer seemed to have all the advantages. He was a nationally known civil rights leader, with impressive oratorical skills. He had a larger war chest and a well-oiled machine, and he was a man, basing his campaign on black masculinity. He attracted publicity and celebrity endorsements. More than fourteen hundred people attended a benefit performance at the Brooklyn Academy of Music headlined by actors Sidney Poitier and Brock Peters; musicians and singers including Lionel Hampton, Mahalia Jackson, and Nina Simone; and Gary, Indiana, mayor Richard Hatcher. For the first time in its history, national CORE endorsed a political candidate—Farmer.

He also had some negatives. His main residence was in Harlem. Much of the community—white and black, Democrat and Republican, male and female—resented him as an interloper. Chisholm believed that the Republicans' choice of Farmer was a slap in the face for Brooklynites. "It was saying to them, you don't have anybody worthwhile." He did not know the Twelfth Congressional District, and as the president of national CORE, he had had difficult relations with Brooklyn CORE, which presented problems winning the black activist vote. Finally, he was running on the Republican Party ticket.

The Chisholm-Farmer race reflected the gains made by African Americans over the previous thirty years, for both candidates were products of the civil rights movement north and south. Politically, they had few differences. Both opposed the war in Vietnam, supported welfare rights, and were critical of the limitations of the War on Poverty. In addition, both supported community control of the schools and in particular were on the side of the community during the Ocean Hill–Brownsville struggle. But the similarities ended there. Whereas Farmer had risen to national prominence through the southern civil rights movement, Chisholm had been born in Brooklyn and was well connected to the West Indian community. Although she was not nationally known, she had earned her nomination through hard work, first in neighborhood activism and then in local and state politics.

Farmer's aggressive, masculinist campaign emphasized the gender differences. His literature argued for a "strong man's image." Chisholm might be a nice woman, he would say, but the Twelfth District needs "a man's voice" in Washington. These tactics offended Chisholm. "He toured the district with sound trucks manned by young dudes with afros, beating tom-toms: the big, black male image," she wrote in her autobiography. She walked into one campaign meeting only to be heckled, "Here comes the Black matriarch!"

Like many other African American women involved in political struggles, Chisholm was acutely aware of how black women were made invisible or cast as the historic stereotypes of Mammies, Jezebels, or Sapphires. Daniel Patrick Moynihan, a Harvard sociologist, adviser to Lyndon Johnson, and, later, US Senator from New York, gave these racially gendered stereotypes academic social science credentials. His inflammatory 1965 report *The Negro Family: The Case for National Action* argued that the primary cause of the "tangle of pathology" in the black community was the matriarchal nature of the black family. Moynihan asserted that the dominant black mother emasculated the black man. The report was criticized by feminists as well as many African Americans, male and female; nonetheless, it was accepted as a serious analysis of the problems of racism and a blueprint for policy proposals that particularly sought to penalize black mothers and demonize black women activists.

The African American community and, in particular, the Black Nationalist struggle did not challenge many of these racial and gendered stereotypes. Women were constantly marginalized in the civil rights movement. Dorothy Height, the leader of the National Council of Negro Women, complained bitterly about the lack of leadership positions for women in the various civil rights organizations. She was the only leader among the major civil rights organizations who was not allowed to speak at the 1963 March on Washington. Pauli Murray, a lawyer and feminist who had staged the first sit-in at a Washington restaurant during World War II, complained, "Not a single woman was invited to make one of the major speeches or be part of the delegation of leaders who went to the White House. The omission was deliberate."[13] Many of the radical Black Nationalist organizations were consciously masculinist. They would not allow women in leadership positions and often used revolutionary rhetoric to maintain traditional gender roles: "The black woman's role is to make babies for the revolution." During the Chisholm-Farmer campaign, both Height and Murray initiated letter-writing campaigns protesting Farmer's demeaning attacks on black women.

Chisholm understood that Farmer was using this rhetoric against her: "To the black men—even some of those supporting me—sensitive about female domination, they were running me down as a bossy female, a would-be matriarch." At this time when the assumption was that black women's activism and Black Nationalism were irreconcilable, Chisholm's campaign demonstrated that it was possible to wage a campaign that brought ordinary women front and center, and at the same time mobilize inclusively for greater social justice.

Television and print media ignored her altogether, another galling aspect of the sexism she endured. An NBC weekend special, *The Campaign and the Candidates,* reported only on Farmer, without even mentioning Chisholm. Even the liberal alternative weekly *Village Voice* ignored her campaign. In frustration, she called the local radio and television stations, only to be told that Farmer had a national reputation, he was newsworthy, and his campaign was more colorful. The manager of one station sneered, "Who are you? A little school teacher who happened to go to the Assembly." The *New York Times* erased her altogether with the headline "Farmer and Woman in Lively Bedford-Stuyvesant Race." Only Gabe Pressman, a local

NBC reporter, spent time with the Chisholm campaign. Escorted to housing projects to talk to potential voters by Conrad Chisholm, he became convinced that Farmer was not going to win.

Despite what seemed like insurmountable obstacles, Mac Holder and Chisholm were confident of victory. Above all, she planned to mobilize the women in the district and turn Farmer's male chauvinist campaign strategy against him. His hyper–Black Nationalist rhetoric offended many women in the community, especially since Farmer had a white wife. "Men always underestimate women," Chisholm wrote. "They underestimated me and they underestimated the women like me." She went into the projects, attended community meetings, and organized her car caravans, which stopped on busy streets, using her gender as her campaign weapon. "I am a woman and you are a woman, and let's show Farmer that woman-power can beat him."

Chisholm knew that the women of Bedford-Stuyvesant were already capable leaders, always organizing something—a parent-teacher association, a civic club, a church social, or a social club. Proud of his wife, Conrad Chisholm explained, "Women are fierce about Shirley. She can pick up the phone and call two hundred women and they'll be here in an hour."[14] But while she made a concerted appeal to women and the historic importance of electing the first black woman to Congress, she also campaigned on her record as an effective state legislator and on what she would do in Congress. She reminded her audiences that they had to judge candidates on their records, not on their gender. Finally, she used humor to shore up her persona as a strong, independent fighter for her community: "They call me Fighting Shirley Chisholm. My mother tells me I was born fighting. I was kicking so hard in the womb she knew I was aching to get out and fight."[15]

Chisholm had another advantage over Farmer: her fluency in Spanish, which had been her minor at Brooklyn College. She was more confident of winning the Puerto Rican neighborhoods than the African American ones. Campaigning in Spanish, she was particularly welcomed in the Puerto Rican neighborhoods, and on election day she decisively carried those areas.

She and Farmer held a number of debates, and each believed she or he came out on top. Farmer had a commanding presence, on and off the stage. Chisholm, small and bespectacled, looked like the schoolteacher she was. But once she got up to speak, she was transformed. She seemed to grow in height. Her voice was clear and confident, and it carried. Furthermore, having lived in Bedford-Stuyvesant all her life, she was able to articulate the community's needs and issues far better than Farmer.

Farmer was convinced the election was in the bag—until the week of the election when he walked through the streets of the Twelfth District, stopping in barbershops, beauty parlors, bars, and pool halls. Only then did he realize he would lose. In the November election, Chisholm outpolled Farmer 2.5 to 1 to win, with 34,885 votes. Even though he ran on both the Republican and Liberal Party tickets, he received only 13,777 votes. The Conservative candidate got 3,771. Farmer, who later became friends with Chisholm and believed that she had "performed well" in Congress, was somewhat chagrined and perhaps a bit bitter about his loss. In his autobiography, he ruefully commented that he now "had a most unique distinction: I was the first black man in U.S. history to be defeated by a woman in a congressional race."[16]

The next day, the *New York Times* front page reported the outcome of the Twelfth Congressional District race. And this time they could not ignore the name of the winner—Shirley Chisholm.

7

An Unquiet Congresswoman

Shirley Chisholm's electoral triumph pushed her into the national spotlight. The headline on the front page of the *New York Times* proclaimed, "First Negro Woman Wins House Seat." A follow-up story quoted Chisholm promising not to be "a quiet freshman Congressman." Another *Times* reporter, Lisa Hammel, discovered a different angle to the Chisholm story: she headlined her article "It Takes Special Kind of Man to Be Congresswoman's Husband," about the importance of married women legislators having spousal endorsement.

Chisholm's victory was reported in countless other publications, including *Ebony* and even *Vogue*. In the two weeks following the election, she was bombarded with requests for interviews. Almost every black newspaper wanted to tell her story. The "women's pages" of the newspapers wanted to report on the "woman's angle," as did a number of international papers. Exhausted after the campaign and the whirlwind of media attention, the Chisholms left for a three-week vacation in Jamaica to rest and enable Shirley to gain back the seventeen pounds she had lost as a result of her operation and her campaigning. But her celebrity preceded her there, and she found herself again surrounded by well-wishers and the media. Everyone, it seemed, wanted to shake her hand and wish her luck.

She arrived in Washington with Conrad in December to start setting up an efficient organization. Immediately, she had to make a number of decisions regarding her staff. Chisholm knew she needed competent, loyal staffers who knew their way around Congress and Washington, DC. Many new representatives hired their campaign workers as well as loyal supporters from their home districts. Resisting pressure from some of her constituents who wanted her to have an all-black staff, Chisholm decided to do something different. Aware that the majority of congressional staffers were women, "intelligent, Washington-wise, college trained—and attractive—young women who do most of the work that make a congressman look good, but often get substandard pay for it and have little hope of advancing to a top staff job," she hired *only* women.[1] Joseph Resnik, a New York Democrat who had not run for reelection, recommended a number of women from his staff. Chisholm hired Travis Kane, an African American from Texas, as her administrative assistant. Shirley Downs, a young white woman with an uproariously bawdy sense of humor from upstate New York, was her legislative assistant, and Karen McRorey, also white, handled Chisholm's constituent services. Carolyn Jones, a black woman, came from the offices of Representative Charles Whalen of Ohio. College students often interned in her office in the Longworth Building as well.

Chisholm also maintained a well-organized office in Brooklyn, largely through the efforts of Wesley McDonald Holder. Over the years, she hired male staffers both in her Brooklyn office and in Washington, but she wanted to begin with women. She was very proud of her staff, and they in turn loved and protected her. They even took responsibility for her wardrobe. "I have a young staff that selects my clothes for me," she explained in an interview. "They don't want me to look old fashioned." But, Chisholm added, "Although I am older than all my staff members, they have a hard time keeping up with me."[2]

A bonus of becoming a congresswoman was that Chisholm was able to realize the Barbadian dream of owning a brownstone; a nineteenth-century terraced row house, which was not uncommon (as well as affordable) in Chisholm's Bedford-Stuyvesant neighborhood. One of the last acts of the Ninetieth Congress was to raise congressional salaries from $30,000 to $42,500, giving the Chisholms unexpected extra income that enabled them to look for a home. Their experience with racist real estate dealings in Brooklyn typified what many of their African American neighbors went through. She and Conrad had saved money to purchase a home. After the 1968 election, the Chisholms were confident that they could now settle down. They found the perfect house, but when they tried to make the purchase the real estate agent suddenly and inexplicably told them the house was unavailable. A week later, the seemingly frightened agent came to them, asking why Chisholm had not mentioned that she was a member of Congress. Chisholm rebuked the real estate agent "in the strongest language," as she put it. Then she and Conrad purchased another house, a nine-room attached row home on St. John's Place, just a few blocks from their rented home.

In 1970 the New York Assembly redrew the congressional districts, and their new home fell one block outside their district line. Chisholm semiseriously wondered whether some opponent in Albany had redrawn the line after she bought the house. This redistricting did not affect her ability to serve in the US Congress. She reflected on her experience:

> The fact that I ran into racism when I tried to buy a house, even in Brooklyn, even after I had been elected to Congress, is significant. But if I had no trouble that would have meant nothing, because my position could make me an exception. For the bars to be let down a little for me here and there has no relevance to most of my brothers and sisters. This brings me back to the point that for there to be real progress for us, we must all move ahead together, and we must do it ourselves.[3]

Chisholm flew home from Washington each weekend, spending every Friday night in her Brooklyn congressional office, listening to her constituents' concerns. People came in asking for help with getting jobs, fighting discrimination in housing, or fighting unjust imprisonment. Local social service agencies constantly lobbied her to save existing services or to secure federal grants to create more services. Saturdays were reserved for entertaining friends. The Chisholms were very sociable and loved going out to dinner and to parties. Sundays they went to church and then back to Washington. She had no time to spend cleaning, decorating, and organizing the domestic chores at her Brooklyn home and was moved when the women in her community volunteered to help out. Occasionally, she participated in larger New York City events. In September 1969, at the first-ever official African American Day Parade held in Harlem, she rode in the lead car with Adam Clayton Powell; both greeted the crowds with the Black Power clenched-fist salute.

Chisholm's congressional office soon became the adopted office for residents of the capital. Until 1971 the District of Columbia had no formal representation in Congress. Then in 1970, President Nixon signed a bill giving the district one nonvoting delegate. Longtime civil rights activist Walter Fauntroy, with the support of local pastors and his friend Coretta Scott King, won the first election for that position. But until then, the overwhelmingly African American residents of Washington, DC, poured into Shirley Chisholm's office with requests, concerns, and complaints similar to those of her Bedford-Stuyvesant constituents: better street lighting, more job-training programs, more police patrols, greater government assistance to children and the poor. She saved Saturday night for Conrad and herself, but found herself surrounded by well-wishers if they went out to dinner or dancing. The Chisholms ended up staying at home Saturday nights.

Chisholm rented a furnished apartment in Washington, but it was burgled one weekend when she was in Brooklyn. All the clothes she had bought to wear in Congress were stolen. The theft made the news, and the notoriety led Chisholm to decide that she wanted her home in Washington to be a refuge from the press. She unlisted her address and phone number.

She was as much in demand by the media in Washington as she had been in Brooklyn, if not more so. Everyone wanted to interview the first black congresswoman—the Washington press, the international press, the black press, student newspapers, and radio and television reporters. She loved one headline, "First Black Woman Will 'Sock It' to Congress." One television reporter wanted to film Chisholm ironing in her kitchen! Chisholm refused that interview.

Before being sworn into Congress, she was inducted into another prestigious organization, the Delta Sigma Theta Sorority, founded January 13, 1913, by twenty-two collegiate women at Howard University who wanted to use their collective strength to promote academic excellence and to provide assistance to persons in need. Their first public act was to participate in the 1913 Women's Suffrage March in Washington, DC. In 1969 the Brooklyn chapter of Delta Sigma Theta hosted the sorority's annual Founders Luncheon. They invited Chisholm to give the keynote speech and swore her in as a member beforehand. Other notable Deltas at the time included Dorothy Height, president of the National Council of Negro Women (and one of Chisholm's idols and role models),and Mary Church Terrell, activist and adviser to Eleanor Roosevelt. Throughout her life, Chisholm spoke of the honor of being a Delta. "Everyone in Congress tells me I'm just a freshman congressman, and you're supposed to keep quiet as a freshman. I listen sweetly to them and then I say, 'Thank you for your advice gentlemen.' But when I get up there on the floor of Congress, I'm sure you'll understand that I am speaking with the pent-up emotions of the community." The audience was thrilled, especially by Chisholm's concluding statement: "One thing people in New York and Washington are afraid of in Shirley Chisholm is *her mouth.*"[4]

Inauguration day was extraordinarily exciting. Chisholm rented a bus so that her friends, relatives, and neighbors could share in the historic moment when she was inducted as a member of the House of Representatives. So many of her constituents attended that not all of them could get into the chamber to watch her being sworn in. Adam Clayton Powell, the first person of African American descent elected to Congress from New York State, greeted Chisholm by kissing her hand. At one of the parties afterward, she was photographed with outgoing President Lyndon Johnson giving her a bear hug.

Ironically, given how determined she had been to get elected, she arrived late on the first day of the Ninety-First Congress. She had been trying to use what little clout she had to get seats for her supporters in the gallery, without success. When she came into the chamber late, wearing her hat and coat, she was told that she had broken protocol. No representative was allowed to bring a coat and hat on to the House floor. After being formally sworn in, she dared to break protocol again by violating an unwritten rule that junior legislators did not speak to senior House members. She went to ask Speaker of the House John McCormack to reenact her swearing in at a nearby hotel so that everyone who had come from Brooklyn could see the ceremony. McCormack graciously readministered the oath of office.

Chisholm entered Congress with a clear social and political agenda that was far more ambitious than those of most of her liberal colleagues. She envisioned an expanded welfare state; programs for the poor, the unemployed, and underserved children; greater access to higher education; and more federal support for public education and health care. She excoriated middle-class liberals for not understanding the real problems facing the poor and, worse, for excluding the disaffected and disempowered from any meaningful decision making.

Her initial enthusiasm and excitement did not last very long. For one thing, most of her congressional peers were cordial, but aloof. "They stood back from me," she said. "Some of the men thought I had horns in my head." A number of men kept asking, "What does your husband think of all this?" Some congressmen, especially from the South, were downright rude, and one southerner in particular was openly hostile, confronting Chisholm whenever she walked into the House chamber. After asking how she was, he would hiss, "Can you imagine ever making forty-two five [the amount of her congressional salary]?" Or he would snarl, "How do you like making forty-two five?" Finally, Chisholm shot back, "If you can't stand the thought of me making forty-two five, then vanish!" adding, "I'm paving the way for more people like me to make forty-two five."[5]

Being the first African American woman in Congress, while historic, in many ways compounded her feelings of isolation and alienation. Of the ten women in the Ninety-First Congress, the only other woman of color was Patsy Mink of Hawaii, who was Japanese American and the first woman of color to be elected to Congress (in 1965). There were nine African American men in Congress.

Chisholm expressed dismay at the lack of decorum on the part of House members. It was discouraging to witness men giving speeches "of no importance," only for the purpose of having them published in the *Congressional Record*. She was offended by much of the congressional culture and work ethic. The use of travel junkets disgusted her. So did the gender segregation in the House spectator's gallery. She was appalled by the contemptuous way many congressmen treated their own staff and constituents. She was outspoken in her opposition to and contempt for the seniority—or, as she called it, "the senility"—system. To Chisholm, the rules of seniority were archaic, racist, and retrograde: "The seniority system keeps a handful of old men, many of them southern whites hostile to every progressive trend, in control of the Congress. These old men stand implacably across the paths that could lead us to a better future. But worse than they, I think, are the majority of members of both houses who continue to submit to the senility system. Apparently, they hope they, too, will grow to be old."[6] She further pointed out that the seniority system all but chained younger legislators to older representatives. They could not speak out for fear of reprisals, could not be independent thinkers, and had to vote as instructed by senior legislators. As a result, they lived in a state of apprehension, until of course they accrued enough seniority to impose their will on their junior colleagues. For Chisholm, the thought of spending another twenty years in Congress before speaking out was unthinkable.

She risked even more political and social isolation when she ignored commonly accepted rules of conduct for a first-year legislator. For example, she dared to protest her first committee assignment. Committees are central to the life of the House, for it is only through them that bills reach the floor of Congress with the possibility of being enacted into law. When Chisholm entered Congress, committee chairs were all-powerful, and their positions were based upon seniority, as were committee assignments. In the Ninety-First Congress, the majority of the committee chairs were southern white men, most of whom remained loyal to Jim Crow and segregation. Although newly elected members of the House could list their preference for committee assignments, they understood that they were very unlikely to get it.

Chisholm wanted to be on the Education and Labor Committee. She knew there were open seats on that committee and reasoned that she was an educator and had served on the Education Committee in Albany. Her second choice was Banking and Currency because it controlled the purse strings for housing construction—and along with education, housing was desperately needed by her constituents. Her third choice was the Post Office and Civil Service Committee, a logical choice given the large numbers of African Americans employed by the post office. She also indicated that she would be amenable to assignment to the Government Operations Committee, for she would have liked to understand better the workings of the federal government and how federal moneys were allocated.

Through the congressional grapevine, she found out that she had been assigned to the Agriculture Committee. At first, she thought this was ridiculous. Then she learned that this committee had jurisdiction over food stamps, surplus food, and migrant labor, subjects that concerned her, so she thought she could make a positive contribution. But then she discovered she had been put on the Rural Development and Forestry Committee, which had absolutely nothing to do with her areas of expertise or the needs of her constituents. For the second time, she challenged House protocol by asking John McCormack to reassign her to a committee that had some relevance to her district. "Mrs. Chisholm, this is the way it is," McCormack explained. "You have to be a good soldier," and he promised that if she was, after a few years she would get her reward. Chisholm was not going to accept this answer. "All my forty-three years I have been a good soldier . . . and I can't be a good soldier anymore," she told him, and then explained that putting a black woman from an urban district on a forestry subcommittee was a waste of her talents. She further threatened, "If you do not assist me, I will have to do my own thing."

Concerned about what Chisholm's "own thing" might be, McCormack contacted the all-powerful Arkansas Democrat Wilbur Mills, chair of the influential House Ways and Means Committee, who was annoyed but nevertheless asked Agriculture Committee chair W. R. Poage of Texas if she could change committees. According to Chisholm, Poague "really blew his stack" at the thought of a junior congressperson challenging a committee assignment. He refused to make the change.

Chisholm had one last avenue of appeal: to make a motion on the House floor that her committee assignment be reconsidered. She had been warned that Wilbur Mills would probably not even allow her to do this, and indeed every time Chisholm stood to be recognized, two or three more senior representatives would stand up, and because they had seniority, they got called on. After six or seven attempts to be recognized, Chisholm walked down to the "well," the open area near the House Speaker's dais, and explained to Mills why she vehemently rejected her committee assignment. She repeated the arguments she had made to McCormack and argued further that because there were so few black congressional representatives, they should be put on committees where they could best represent their constituents. After more procedural wrangling, Mills finally found a parliamentary procedure to allow her to make her motion, which passed, and Chisholm won her first congressional battle.

Eventually, she was reassigned to the Veterans Affairs Committee, which pleased her. "There are a lot more veterans in my district than there are trees," as she put it.[7] Olin (Tiger) Teague of Texas, the chair of the House Democratic Caucus and of the House Committee on Veterans Affairs—one of the few congressmen to treat Chisholm with collegiality and generosity—offered to put her on the Education and Training Subcommittee, whose jurisdiction covered areas in which she had considerable interest and expertise.

Chisholm considered this her first victory. She was proud of the editorial support she received from the Washington press, the *New York Daily News,* and some suburban newspapers such as the *Rockland County (NY) Journal News.* At the same time, many of her congressional colleagues made it very clear that they disapproved of and resented this upstart African American woman. Adam Clayton Powell, who throughout his congressional career had been plagued by attempts to undermine and discredit him, warned Chisholm to be more careful and not so outspoken. Like her determined stand when she first arrived in Albany, Chisholm wanted to make her mark as a person of courage and independence, one who would put the needs of her constituents before those congressional representatives as well as congressional protocol.

True to character, she did not take Powell's advice. As soon as she received her new committee assignment, Chisholm announced she would vote no on every bill before the House that provided money for the Department of Defense. This was both a statement against the US war in Vietnam and a protest of the war's effects on the people in her district. During her campaign, she had spoken out against the war and its devastating impact on the people of Brooklyn but had never participated in antiwar demonstrations. Like so many of her constituents, she believed the war was colonialist and racist. When she entered Congress in January 1969, the antiwar movement was at its peak, yet, as she admitted, opposition to the war was ninth on her list of legislative and political priorities. At this point, she was somewhat optimistic that President Nixon would fulfill his promise of ending the war and providing the necessary funds for rebuilding the cities. That hope was soon dashed, as Nixon's political ambitions and priorities became clear.

In March 1969, Nixon announced that his administration would increase military spending to build an Anti-Ballistic Missile System and at the same time that the District of Columbia's antipoverty program Operation Head Start would be cut for lack of funds. That was too much for Chisholm, who had been advocating on behalf of President Johnson's antipoverty programs. She decided to devote her maiden speech in Congress to explaining why she planned to vote against every defense funding bill until Congress began to vote for programs providing jobs and social welfare. Referring to herself as a teacher and a woman, she said, "As I take this stand today I am joined by every mother, wife and widow in this land who ever asked herself why the generals can play with billions while families crumble under the weight of hunger, sickness and unemployment." She concluded, "We must force this administration to rethink its distorted, unreal state of priorities. Our children, our jobless men, our deprived, rejected and starving fellow citizens must come first. For this reason I intend to vote 'no' on every money bill that comes to the floor of this House . . . until our country starts to use its strength, its tremendous resources for people and peace, not for profits and war."[8]

The speech was bold, daring, intentionally provocative, and direct. However, as she ruefully reflected later, it had absolutely no impact. No one in Congress was ever swayed by speeches, let alone even listening to their colleagues' points of view. As she walked back to her seat, she overheard one member whisper to another, "You know that she's crazy." Others told her she should not be making antiwar speeches in a time of war; still others explained that even if she had a valid point, it was not good politics to vote against defense spending. Chisholm found these reactions particularly discouraging. At that time, the majority of Americans wanted a way out of the fighting, but politicians were too cowardly to try to find one.

Chisholm also tried to mount a campaign against the emergency section of the preventive detention section of the Internal Security Act, whose provisions included the confinement of possible spies and saboteurs in the case of war or domestic insurrection. She perceived it as being used mainly in a racist way. Addressing Congress, she pointed out that that particular section of the Internal Security Act of 1952 was particularly offensive to Americans of color. "It was not the Italians and Germans who were rounded up in 1942 under a presidential order, but the Japanese-Americans who were easily identifiable because of the color of their skin." Referring to the policy of the Federal Bureau of Investigation (FBI) of targeting black militants, she concluded, "Today it is not the Ku Klux Klan or the [crime] Syndicate whose doors are being kicked in, it is the Black Panthers. Skin, skin, skin color, gentlemen, that's the criteria. It makes us special targets."[9]

Although Chisholm was committed to working for profound social change within the confines of the existing political system, she was not politically naive. Aware that social movements and strong organizations were of great importance in effecting social change and influencing Congress, she founded, joined, and led many organizations that played a pivotal role in social justice issues—both within government and without. She worked with male African American legislators to organize the Congressional Black Caucus, which over the years emerged as a highly visible and often effective organization speaking on behalf of African Americans. Prior to 1969, there had been sporadic attempts to bring African American legislators together to work on common issues. Nixon's election moved the process along. One of the black legislators' first public actions as a group was to protest the nomination of Clement Haynsworth, a federal appeals court judge with extreme antilabor and prosegregation rulings, to the US Supreme Court. Their second action, in 1969, was to conduct an unofficial hearing on the killing of Black Panther leader Fred Hampton by Chicago police. Many civil rights activists and former attorney general Ramsey Clark believed that the Chicago Police Department was in violation of federal civil rights laws. In February 1970, black representatives wrote a letter to Nixon, requesting a meeting to discuss a wide range of issues concerning black and poor people in the United States. Nixon refused to acknowledge the letter for fourteen months. In protest, the African American delegation staged a boycott of his State of the Union address and immediately afterward renamed themselves the Congressional Black Caucus. When they finally met with Nixon in 1971, they presented sixty recommendations for government actions to address domestic and foreign policy issues.

More important, the CBC described itself as representing African Americans: "Our concerns and obligations as members of Congress do not stop at the boundaries of our districts, our concerns are national and international in scope. We are petitioned by citizens living hundreds of miles from our districts who look upon us as Congressmen-at-large for black people and poor people in the United States."[10] Chisholm, the first female member of the caucus, had a difficult relationship with many of her black male colleagues during much of her congressional career. Part of the reason was that the men in the caucus shared similar male chauvinist outlooks as did white congressmen. Also, Chisholm, who did not take orders from or allow herself to be bossed around by white congressmen, took the same attitude toward her black colleagues.

While reflecting the politics and passions of the traditional urban liberalism of her Brooklyn constituency, Chisholm also began to identify herself more and more with the burgeoning women's movement and feminism. It was a slow process that initially grew out of her admiration for her strong, struggling grandmother, great-aunt, and mother and her relationships with the black women in her neighborhood, at Brooklyn College, and in her assembly district and congressional constituencies. In her campaigns both for the state legislature and for Congress, she called upon the women in her district to support her and received that support. In Albany she supported women's rights and women's social benefits as well as a right to abortion. The campaign that elected her to Congress brought gender to the fore, focusing on the importance of black women's leadership.

Beginning in 1969, Chisholm stepped forward as a leader of mainstream feminism and as the most outspoken feminist in the Congress. In *Unbought and Unbossed,* she pointed out that those women "can have equal treatment if they will fight for it, and they are starting to organize." She understood that changing discriminatory laws would not be enough to win equality. "Women must do it themselves. They must become revolutionaries."[11]

At the same time, Chisholm brought her class and racial understanding to all the issues the women's movement was raising. "I'm not a burn the bra kind of women's liberationist," she explained in an interview. "I've been liberated a long time." She continued, "There's some aspects of women's liberation that relate to Black women, but the rest of it is baloney." For example, "If the women's liberation movement persists in fighting for a national day care system, then this is important." An example of "baloney" was Betty Friedan's asking Chisholm to join a group of women picketing a men's-only cocktail lounge. "Well that's a white, middle-class virtue. If men don't want me in their lounges, I don't want to be in them."[12]

Nevertheless, Chisholm used her celebrity in Congress to support the women's movement and advocate for gender equality. Only recently has the formative, influential role she played in the women's movement, and her lasting legacy in it, been recognized. African American feminist activists like Chisholm challenged the dominant narrative that the women's movement was entirely white and focused only on middle-class women's issues. It was Chisholm who on August 10, 1970, reintroduced in the House of Representatives the Equal Rights Amendment, which had first been brought to Congress in 1923 by former suffragist and National Women's Party president Alice Paul. Chisholm's sponsorship of and support for the ERA were of great significance because as a champion of racial justice, she was able to connect gender, race, and social equality on a national scale.

Chisholm consistently brought her particular perspective as a black working-class daughter of immigrants into all the legislation she proposed. For example, she supported the demands of the National Council on Household Employment (NCHE). Founded by middle-class white women in the 1960s, its purpose was to train women for domestic work and to educate employers in how to better working conditions. By 1970, led by African American women, the NCHE began to demand that housework be recognized as regular employment and that household workers' labor be recognized as equal to other categories of employment and given legal protection. Just as many white feminists sought to "liberate" themselves from housewifery and thus dependence on their husbands, Chisholm understood that setting a minimum wage for domestics and unionizing them would reduce their dependence on their employers (usually white women). She maintained that a minimum wage for domestics could alleviate the burden of poverty on black families, 50 percent of which were headed by a woman. "Of those poor female heads of households who work, over half worked as maids in 1970 and had incomes under the poverty line." Furthermore, Chisholm reminded Congress how domestic labor contributes to the economic life of the country because the purchase and use of household cleaning products and appliances benefit the economy. "Every household product used by a domestic from Handy-Andy to a Hoover, is a product which has moved in interstate commerce." When conservative congressmen painted a picture of women being incapable of processing and maintaining the necessary employment records for domestic workers, Chisholm angrily explained the nature of women's work in the home:

> This may come as a shock to Members of this House, but in most homes it is the wife who handles the family budget, and bookkeeping. She can tell you how much you owe at the bank, on the car loan, the charges run up on her credit cards, and in these days of spiraling food prices, she has been doing plenty of fancy figuring about base prices at the grocery store. To suggest that women do not know how to add and subtract is an insult to women and totally contrary to all existing evidence.[13]

By the end of her first term, she had become a leading public spokesperson on the issue of women's rights and one of the very few who connected class, race, and gender with all women's lives. She constantly tried to build coalitions between mainstream feminists and women of color, arguing that such coalitions could potentially be very powerful in forcing social change. For someone who called upon women to become "revolutionaries," she attracted a wide mainstream audience, even appearing in the August 1970 issue of *McCall's*, a popular woman's magazine, in an article titled "A Visiting Feminine Eye: I'd Rather Be Black than Female."[14]

Consistent with her belief that outside organization was imperative to pressure legislators to enact meaningful social change, she founded or joined a wide range of women's organizations, including the National Organization for Women and the Women's Action Alliance, whose mission was "to assist women working on practical, local action projects; projects that attack the special problems of social dependence, discrimination, and limited life alternatives they face because they are women."

She was a longtime member of the National Council of Negro Women, and with the emergence of black feminist consciousness she also joined the Coalition of 100 Black Women and the National Black Feminist Organization. In July 1971, she joined with prominent feminists Gloria Steinem, Bella Abzug, and Betty Friedan to found the National Women's Political Caucus (NWPC). Explaining why she supported such an organization, Chisholm stated, "We are no longer going to be the silent majority and watch quietly what is happening to the United States." Here Chisholm played a pivotal role in challenging the NWPC to take up the concerns of women of color. The NWPC established three main issues to advocate for: reproductive freedom, affordable child care, and passage of the Equal Rights Amendment. It also addressed issues of income inequality and developing diversity at all levels of political leadership. At the founding meeting, African American women made up 10 percent of the audience. Speaking for them, Chisholm asked that the NWPC go on record that it would not support any candidate, male or female, who held racist views, even if that candidate supported women's rights.

The NWPC delegates voted unanimously never to support racist candidates. Two years later, she again addressed the NWPC, pointing out the ways in which white women benefited from racial privilege. Her goal was to broaden the feminist movement by bringing in more women of color, poor women, and working-class women. Unfortunately, the schisms of difference and mistrust between the experiences of mainstream feminists and women of color were too difficult to overcome in the NWPC.[15] In a presentation at Brooklyn College, Gloria Steinem recounted Chisholm's influence on her appearance at the NWPC founding. At Chisholm's suggestion, Steinem forswore her trademark blue jeans and black turtleneck sweater in favor of what Chisholm believed was more appropriate—a dress.

Chisholm constantly encouraged other women of color to join feminist organizations. Praising civil rights activist Fannie Lou Hamer for her work with the NWPC, she enthused that "for the first time in a movement such as this, we had many Blacks participating. 'She added that the NWPC "came from all classes, all colors and all political persuasions." She also constantly confronted the prevailing racial assumptions of white feminist leaders and challenged these women's organizations to prioritize the needs of the poor and women of color.

She was a sought-after speaker. In June 1969, the Women's Political Action Committee invited Chisholm to speak in Detroit, Michigan. Rosa Parks, the legendary civil rights activist, introduced her as a "pepper pot," a southern expression for a feisty woman, and praised her "defiance and loyalty to her constituents," referring to her refusal to sit on the Agriculture Committee. Parks also admired Chisholm's "aggressive and determined attitude [that] landed her on the veterans committee where she fought hard to end segregation in the military." Parks also saw a kinship with Chisholm, in that both had loving and supportive husbands who did not mind that their wives were in the spotlight.[16]

One of her most courageous acts was her public support for legalized abortion, a position that put her at odds with the leaderships of both the traditional civil rights organizations and the more militant Black Nationalist movement. Most men (and some women) in the black struggle were vehemently anti–birth control and antiabortion, charging that these were tools of white America to commit genocide against African Americans. Many argued further that the role of women in the black revolution was to bring black revolutionaries into the world. However, these nationalists did not take into account the actual lives of black women. Where abortion was illegal, black women tried to get abortions in disproportionately larger numbers than did white women, and consequently also died in disproportionate numbers from illegal abortions.

In *Unbought and Unbossed,* Chisholm titled one chapter "Facing the Abortion Question." In a very measured essay, she explained how her thinking had evolved from partial support for abortion rights to calling for a repeal of all restrictive abortion laws. Anchored as she was in the reality of her female constituents' lives, Chisholm explained that abortion, right or wrong, was a fact of life. Given that tens of thousands of women terminated pregnancies, abortion should not be criminalized. For Chisholm, the choice was simple: "what kind of abortions society wants women to have—clean competent ones performed by competent physicians or septic, dangerous ones done by incompetent practitioners." She asserted that abortion rights and family planning should be an integral component of women's overall medical care, regardless of class, marital status, or age. She also took on the issue of genocide, arguing, "To label family planning and legal abortion programs 'genocide' is male rhetoric, for male ears," and reminded her readers that in 1969, "49% of the deaths of pregnant black women and 65 percent of those of Puerto Rican women were due to criminal, amateur abortions."[17]

In 1969, asked to become honorary president of the National Association for the Repeal of Abortion Laws (now known as NARAL Pro-Choice America), she accepted. As the only African American woman in Congress, and very aware of her symbolic as well as her political status, Chisholm proposed abortion legislation in Congress and supported the New York State Legislature's repeal of that state's restrictive abortion laws in 1970. She continued her efforts to promote birth control and abortion rights, but with little success. Chisholm got very little support from her colleagues, who found excuse after excuse not to take a stand. "This is not the time," one would explain. A few would promise to support legislation, but not until it got out of committee and onto the House floor. A few flatly refused, saying, "This kind of trouble, I don't need." In 1973 the Supreme Court settled the issue—temporarily—with the *Roe v. Wade* decision, which gave women the constitutional right to abortion.[18]

In Congress Chisholm almost always voted with the Democratic Party. But in 1969, she bucked the New York City Democratic machine by not supporting the machine-backed Democratic candidate for mayor. This move by Chisholm would have national implications, especially in shoring up her credentials as a politician who followed her beliefs and not the party bosses. Her decision to support John V. Lindsay, a liberal Republican, also demonstrated that Chisholm was a shrewd, strategic political thinker who understood the needs of her constituents. In 1965 Lindsay had been elected mayor. By 1969 a conservative backlash against Lindsay caused him to lose the Republican mayoral primary to conservative state senator John Marchi. The Democratic nominee was the equally conservative city controller, Mario Procaccino. Lindsay was still on the ballot as the candidate of the New York Liberal Party. As a Democrat, Chisholm was expected to support the Democrat. However, the Republican Lindsay had demonstrated greater understanding of the problems of New York City's poor than had Procaccino. "He seemed cut from the same cloth as the Republican nominee, a reactionary in the strict sense of the word," Chisholm wrote.[19] Her closest advisers, including her husband and Wesley McDonald Holder, urged her not to support Lindsay, but in the end Chisholm vigorously campaigned for him, and her support proved critical for his reelection. African Americans and Puerto Ricans, who were concentrated in Harlem, the South Bronx, and various Brooklyn neighborhoods—including Bedford-Stuyvesant and Brownsville—voted overwhelmingly for Lindsay. Close to election day, Percy Sutton and Adam Clayton Powell, two of the most prominent black Democrats in New York, finally joined Chisholm in endorsing and campaigning for Lindsay.

As expected, the white male Democratic Party leadership was furious with Chisholm. Procaccino and the Westchester Democratic

Club threatened to unseat her as a national committeewoman, a prestigious and influential post within the Democratic Party. Chisholm fought back, reminding them that in a similar but not identical situation, no one had asked President Franklin Roosevelt to resign his office when he supported Republican Fiorello La Guardia for mayor in 1930. Some black New York City Democratic Party leaders told her she no longer had a future in Democratic Party politics. But once again, Chisholm displayed greater understanding of the pulse of her constituents than these party leaders. The *Amsterdam News,* which supported Lindsay, praised Chisholm's bravery and independence, calling her the black Joan of Arc. She did not lose her national committeewoman seat, and when she ran for reelection in 1970 she received both the Democratic and the Liberal Party endorsements. She told the press she was not actively campaigning because her political opponents did not seriously threaten her. She was right. On November 5 she received 82 percent of the vote.

In two years, Chisholm had gone from an unknown local Brooklyn Democratic Party activist to one of the most important and influential women in the United States. Riding the crest of the great social movements of the sixties—the civil rights and Black Power movements, the anti–Vietnam War movement, the youth's, women's, and poor people's struggles—she became an articulate spokesperson for these groups and movements. Admired and reviled for being "unbought and unbossed" inside and outside Congress, she demonstrated great political savvy and courage as she fought for her expansive, inclusive political agenda. Even though she did not sponsor any major legislation in her first two years (the only legislation she sponsored that passed gave the District of Columbia the authority to erect a statue to Mary McLeod Bethune), she launched her second term in Congress by promising to speak out even louder about the problems of poverty, unemployment, racial injustice, war, and women's rights.

8

Testing the Presidential Waters

Chisholm began thinking about the possibility of a presidential run as early as 1969. As the sixties drew to a close and a new decade began, conditions seemed very promising for an outspoken supporter of the urban liberal social justice agenda.

First and foremost, Chisholm was much attuned to the social movements of the young and their impact on the rest of US society. Forces often working together marked the seventies. For example, opposition to the war in Vietnam was growing beyond the confines of middle-class youth, even to the white working class and to the military. Vietnam Veterans Against the War, founded in 1967, had a membership of five thousand by 1970. In April 1971, the VVAW organized a peaceful antiwar protest, ending on the Capitol steps, where Chisholm and other congressional supporters including Bella Abzug, Maine senator Edmund Muskie, and the New York congressman Republican Ogden Reid, addressed the large crowd. The militancy of the "New Left," that is, the radical student and antiwar movement, reached its peak after May 1970. Campus unrest exploded in opposition to Nixon's invasion of Cambodia, resulting in the National Guard firing upon and killing four white students at Kent State University in Ohio; in another incident ten days later, police open fired and killed two black students at Jackson State College, now Jackson State University. Both these events sparked widespread outrage, as hundreds of universities, colleges, and high schools closed throughout the United States in a nationwide student strike while hundreds of thousands marched on Washington to protest the war and the killings.

The black struggle, which had lost some of its transformational leaders in the sixties, including Medgar Evers, Malcolm X, and Martin Luther King Jr., was moving in new directions. The largest and arguably most confrontational of the Black Nationalist organizations was the Black Panther Party. Founded in 1966, the Panthers, as they were called, faced tremendous government repression and beginning in the 1970s began to advocate "survival programs" for the black community instead of armed confrontation with the police. The most famous of these was the Free Breakfast for Children Program, initially run out of Oakland Church, which fed thousands of black and Latino schoolchildren.

Chisholm stood alone as a national black elected official in her public support for black militants. For example, she helped raise bail for Black Panther Party member Joan Bird, who at twenty-one was accused of conspiracy to commit murder, beaten while arrested, and spent almost a year and a half in jail before she was acquitted. She explained her support of Joan Bird in the context of the larger social issues. "If you take the incarceration of this young woman in terms of what is happening in our society—when we should be incarcerating those who are bringing narcotics into this country—big organized gamblers and criminals who are being protected in different ways—I think we have to ask whether or not this truly is justice."[1] She was also publicly critical of the arrest and imprisonment of Black Power activist Angela Davis, accused of conspiracy and murder, and supported the "Free Angela" movement. Chisholm was defiantly unapologetic for her support for this kind of militancy, for she understood the rage of so many young black people.

Black and Latino students were now leading the student revolt, demanding admission of more students of color to colleges and universities as well as more black, Latino, Asian, women's, and gender studies programs and centers. Chisholm did not endorse the 1969 actions of the Cornell University students who, outraged at a campus cross burning, felt threatened enough to take up guns to support their demands for an African American studies program, but she supported and arranged for bail for jailed black students at her alma mater, Brooklyn College, who were arrested at a protest demanding black and Latino studies programs—demands she herself had expressed twenty-five years earlier when she was a student activist.

Chisholm's support for militants and militancy was always within the confines of the political system. Concerned about the racism and brutality of the prison system, the majority of whose inmates were black and Latino, she worked with colleagues to address prisoner concerns. She was called in to help address prisoners' demands at a Long Island City, New York, prison uprising. When prisoners at the District of Columbia jail rebelled, taking seventy-eight hostages and threatening to kill them, they demanded to speak with Chisholm. Along with a small group of observers, she went into the dangerous situation, persuaded the prisoners to release the hostages, and then arranged for the prisoners to obtain a hearing for their grievances. In 1973 she took to the floor of Congress to denounce the brutal massacre at Attica Prison, calling it a "national tragedy and disgrace." In September 1971, more than a thousand prisoners at the Attica Correctional facility, in upstate New York, rebelled and seized control of the prison, taking thirty-three staff hostage. After four days of negotiations, New York governor Nelson Rockefeller ordered that state police take control of the prison. After the uprising was brutally suppressed, more than thirty-nine people were dead, including ten correctional officers and civilian employees. All were shot by state police. Along with New York City congressional colleagues Bella Abzug, Herman Badillo, and Ed Koch, she demanded legislation guaranteeing prisoners' basic human rights.

On August 26, 1970, the women's movement organized massive demonstrations across the United States. The Women's Strike for Equality, as it was called, celebrated the fiftieth anniversary of the passing of the Nineteenth Amendment, which effectively gave American women the right to vote. The rally was organized by the National Organization for Women and supported by the more radical women's liberation movement. More than twenty thousand women marched down Fifth Avenue, chanting slogans for equality and liberation.

Demonstrations and rallies were held in numerous other cities. The gathering was the largest on behalf of women in the United States since the days of suffragist protests sixty years before. The demonstrations primarily focused on equal opportunity in the workforce, political rights for women, and social equality in relationships such as marriage. Women also demanded the right to abortion, free child care, and support for lesbian rights (the slogan at the time was freedom of sexual expression). Mainstream feminist leaders who spoke to the crowd included Betty Friedan, Gloria Steinem, and Bella Abzug. Jacqui Ceballos, one of the organizers, was convinced that Chisholm had been invited to speak, but there is no record of her presence. Only one black woman, Eleanor Holmes Norton, then the New York City commissioner for human rights, spoke from the platform.

Chisholm, who learned from her father the importance of labor- and trade-union struggles, was very sympathetic to changes taking place among working-class youth. Chisholm was an active supporter of the successful 1969 Service Employees International Union, Local 1199B Charleston Hospital Workers' Strike, which brought civil rights and women's movement activists together to support the demands of the union. She walked with the United Farmworkers' Organizing Committee, which became the United Farmworkers' Union, in 1972. Working-class people, affected by the youth culture of the 1960s and '70s, also rebelled. The period 1968–1973 was a time of labor militancy, with an increase in both organized and unauthorized (wildcat) strikes. The United Farm Workers of America and the Hospital Workers Local 1199 inspired the New Left, Latino, black, and women's movements to engage in union activism. African American, Latino, women, and lesbian and gay trade unionists formed caucuses within their unions, transformed their unions' traditional women's or fair-practices (read: racial justice) committees, or formed cross union-industry organizations to champion social justice, along with more traditional union demands for better wages and working conditions. Young workers were profoundly discontented with the top-down, overpaid, bureaucratic, old, and often corrupt union leadership. Black Nationalism exploded in the labor movement, beginning in the automobile industry with the organization of the Detroit

Revolutionary Union Movement, which combined union and Black Power militancy. The movement spread to other unionized industries with the formation of the League of Black Revolutionary Workers. The most explosive expression of working-class discontent erupted in March 1970 when more than two hundred thousand postal workers in the West and Northeast participated in the largest wildcat strike in the nation's history. Thirty thousand national guardsmen were called out to break the eight-day walkout. A month later, a national truckers' wildcat strike spread to sixteen cities.

It was against this background that Chisholm took the oath of office for the second time in 1971. She identified with the social upheavals taking place outside the legislative political arena. At the same time, she had already taken one concrete step toward a possible presidential run, and that was the publication of *Unbought and Unbossed* in 1971, six months before Chisholm began her congressional reelection campaign. Publishing a campaign autobiography is a common move for presidential aspirants. However, Chisholm does not go into great detail as to why she wrote the book at this particular time, except to say she hopes she will be remembered "for what I have done, not for what I happen to be. And I hope that my having made it, the hard way, can be some kind of inspiration, particularly to women." Her introduction concludes with her now famous declaration that "of my two 'handicaps' being female put many more obstacles in my path than my being black."

Unbought and Unbossed provided a way for her to introduce herself to the larger public. It is actually much less a straight autobiography than a reflection on the influences on her life and on her struggles, challenges, and successes, plus enough of her personal story to make her appear strong, admirable, and likable. But unlike many presidential-hopeful autobiographies or memoirs, *Unbought* is not filled with platitudes and vague campaign promises. Very few campaign biographies have ever been as blunt and to the point as this one. She is very critical of Congress, the seniority system, white liberals, and many black politicians. She explains her support for feminism, a woman's right to abortion, the youth revolt, and the need to expand the social welfare programs of Johnson's Great Society, as well as her opposition to the masculinism of many Black Nationalists. The book was favorably reviewed by Charlayne Hunter (now Charlayne Hunter-Gault), who wrote, "It is not a literary masterpiece. In fact it reads like a school primer. But it is a testament to her honesty and vigilance."[2]

Chisholm took a slightly less confrontational stance in her second term in office. Perhaps she was thinking of her long-term future as a successful legislator, or she wanted to create allies in anticipation of a presidential run. We may never know; she never explained her shift in tactics. She still wanted to serve on the Education and Labor Committee, but this time, rather than stage another public clash to obtain a seat on it, she chose a more political tactic. She decided not to support liberal Democrat and Congressional Black Caucus member John Conyers. To garner support from two very powerful senior Democrats, she voted for Louisiana congressman Hale Boggs as House majority whip and for the very conservative southerner Joe D. Waggonner Jr. for the House Rules Committee. Chisholm often angered her political supporters when she placed her political ambitions before her political principles.

She decided that, because she had so little seniority in Congress, pursuing her legislative agenda meant she would have to compromise. "I have to be practical," she confided to her husband. "Sometimes you have to give a little in order to get a lot."[3] She modified her position on voting against any defense appropriation bill. Though steadfast in her opposition to the war and support for the antiwar movement, she voted for some defense appropriation bills that were not Vietnam War related. She even began to compromise on some war-related appropriations bills, if their supporters supported legislation that she was proposing.

Along with the Education and Labor Committee, she was given other committee assignments, one of which was a seat on an eleven-member committee created to study the possibility of reforming the seniority system. House Democrats vetoed the committee's recommendations, but nonetheless enacted a few reforms. In an interview, Chisholm urged young people, "Don't give up yet on the system, we have made improvements."[4] In *Unbought and Unbossed,* she explains that she believed her talent for serving in Congress was not primarily as a legislator. Rather, she wanted to be an advocate, a voice for those whom both Democrats and Republicans ignored. She particularly looked to young people and to the "have-nots—the blacks, browns, reds, yellows and whites" as the agents for change inside and outside the political system. "My role as I see it is to help them do so, working outside of Washington, perhaps as much as in it."[5]

In July 1971, she began more serious discussions about the possibilities of a presidential run with Conrad as well as her trusted adviser Wesley McDonald Holder. Both promised to support her, but pointed out the overwhelming odds against her—lack of money, national recognition, and a well-organized staff, combined with the race and gender bias she would face on a daily basis. In her account of the campaign, *The Good Fight,* she writes that students were the first group to urge her to run. On one occasion, when she explained the hurdles she faced, especially being black and a woman, a student demanded, "When are we going to break this tradition?" That question stayed with her.

Women's groups also urged her to run. Chisholm's interest in the presidency may have been piqued when she heard Betty Friedan declare at the 1971 founding meeting of the National Women's Political Caucus, "It is not so impossible that a woman may run for president in 1976—and win!"[6] Florynce (Flo) Kennedy, a civil rights attorney, political activist, and pioneering second-wave feminist, founded the National Feminist Party in 1971. Her first act was to nominate Chisholm for president. The NFP produced Chisholm's first campaign button, "Ms. Chiz for Pres." Other black women urged her to run. The idea that any woman, black or white, could run for president may have seemed just a pipe dream, possibly because before 1972 only four women had done so, and two of them were members of third or minor political parties. In 1964 Margaret Chase Smith, Republican from Maine, who served in both the House and the Senate, was the first woman from one of the two major political parties to run for the presidency. She did it "to break the barrier against women being seriously considered for the presidency of the United States—to destroy any political bigotry against women on this score."[7] Smith had no illusions that she would win the nomination, but aided by a group of dedicated Republican women, she had her name placed in nomination at the Republican National Convention in San Francisco and received twenty-seven delegate votes. The number of African Americans who had run for president was also small. Prior to 1972, there were only six, and except for Charlene Mitchell, who ran in 1968, on the Communist Party ticket, all were men and all were from minor or third parties.

Chisholm was considering a presidential run at a time when groups were organizing to increase the number of black as well as female voters and elected officials. Members of the Democratic Select Committee, the precursor of the Congressional Black Caucus, had been strategizing around a campaign for increasing the number of black elected officials. By 1970 the CBC was mobilizing constituents in the civil rights movement and black struggles around electoral politics. The passage of the 1965 Voting Rights Act, combined with voter-registration campaigns organized by CORE, the NAACP, and the Student Nonviolent Coordinating Committee, dramatically enlarged the black electorate as well as black representation. From 1964 to 1972, the number of African Americans of voting age increased from 10.3 percent of the population to 13.5 percent. In 1969 there were more than 1,000 African American elected officials, of whom 131 were women. By 1975 the number had tripled. The concentration of African Americans in major urban areas gave rise to hopes for greater electoral gains by African American candidates for office.

However, even after the Supreme Court rulings on redistricting and the Voting Rights Act, African Americans were seriously underrepresented. There were only twelve black members in the House and one in the Senate, Edward Brooke, a Republican from Massachusetts. Except for Ron Dellums from Oakland, California, all African American elected officials came from congressional districts that were overwhelmingly African American. Most metropolitan centers north of the Mason-Dixon line had entrenched political machines created in the nineteenth and early twentieth centuries by white ethnics tied to the Democratic Party. Machine politics kept African Americans from achieving political representation and being elected to office. In the South, segregationists maintained political control. Among the major urban centers, there were only three black mayors.

In early 1970, radical Black Nationalists, such as poet, playwright, and political activist Amiri Baraka, began to make tactical alliances with black members of Congress to discuss the possibilities of a black political party. In particular, they worked with Charles Diggs, who served on the house Committee for African Affairs, and Ron Dellums of Oakland, one of the most left-wing members of Congress at the time. Percy Sutton (then Manhattan Borough president), John Conyers (representative from Michigan), and newly elected Gary, Indiana, mayor Richard Hatcher called a meeting to be held September 24–25, 1971, in Northlake, outside Chicago, for the purpose of translating the ideas of Black Power into an effective electoral strategy. According to historian Manning Marable, this conference was "probably the only instance between 1965 and 1983 when representatives of virtually every tendency of the black movement sat down together in the same room."[8]

Every leader of the black struggle was there, including members of Congress, state legislators, and leaders of the major civil rights organizations. Their goal was to chart the course for the 1972 elections, and everyone who attended had his own specific political agenda. For example, Dr. John Cashin, chair of the Alabama National Democratic Party, brought with him a resolution from the Southern Black Caucuses within the Democratic Party opposing a black presidential candidate, urging all African Americans "to stand aloof from the entire list of candidates for the Presidency of the United States." Percy Sutton advocated for a black presidential candidate, arguing that this would create "a strategy and sense of internal unity which carries far beyond the convention floor and the election of 1972. It carries with it a political awareness that will flow into the local elections of every city, town and village where black people live."[9] Georgia state representative Julian Bond submitted a position paper urging that each state or city with a significant black population run a favorite son or daughter—"a nod to me," Chisholm wrote in reference to Bond's comment—in hopes of mobilizing the black vote and bringing black delegates to the Democratic convention. Another paper suggested that the sixty recommendations sent by the CBC to President Nixon early in 1971 be sent to all the Democratic presidential candidates.

The conference did not end with a unified point of view, but participants agreed to keep on meeting for future discussions.

Chisholm did not attend the conference, but sent her aide Thaddeus Garrett instead. She had good reason not to go, for it seemed that the only thing all the men agreed on was that she should not be the first black candidate for president and that she had no business even stating such an intention. Garrett reported back that the men at the meeting believed that if she ran, she would be the woman's candidate, as opposed to the black candidate. He had answered this concern by pointing out that for Chisholm, class, race, and gender could not be separated. "She is a black woman, of the black experience and from one of the blackest districts in the country. She can do nothing but be black in her dealings."[10] One conference participant told a *Washington Post* reporter, "In this first serious effort of blacks for high political office, it would be better if it were a man."

Julian Bond agreed, in a comment that resonated with Moynihan's image of the black matriarch. "There was anger against her. She thought that by virtue of announcing her candidacy we [black men?] would fall in line. There was enormous resentment at this idea. Politicians like to be asked. She would put it down to sexism and there was some of that." He added, in a remark laced with sexism, "I don't think her gender had as much to do with it as her style." Another unnamed member of the CBC told the *New York Times*, "She's a militant feminist and she rubs us the wrong way."[11] Only Ron Dellums supported her, telling the *Washington Post* reporter, "She could have a dramatic effect on politics in this country. She could bring together the elements necessary to create a third force in American politics and by 1976, we would be able to put together a ticket that could win." But California state assemblyman Willie Brown, who believed that Chisholm would "embarrass the black cause," spent the next six months trying to convince Dellums he was wrong.[12]

A month later, Chisholm was invited to speak at the Black Expo organized by Jesse Jackson's Operation Breadbasket, an organization dedicated to improving the economic conditions of black communities across the United States. Jackson was arguably one of the most influential black leaders at the time. The event highlighted black achievements in business, the arts, and other fields. At a workshop on women in politics where she spoke along with Coretta Scott King, she overheard a black politician comment loudly, "There she is—that little black matriarch who goes around messing things up." Furious, Chisholm focused her anger on warning the workshop audience about the obstacles facing them. She told these one thousand women, most of them African American, that she "dared" to seek the presidency because "we are tired of tokenism and look-how-far-we've-comism" and that it was imperative for black women "to turn this country around."[13] To run for office, she warned, black women needed enough self-confidence not to "be worn down by the sexist attacks that they will have to encounter on top of the racial slurs." Repeating her famous comment that "during twenty years in local ward politics, four as a state legislator and four as a member of Congress, I had met far more discrimination because I am a woman than because I am black." While admitting she was getting carried away, she continued to lash out at the black men who opposed her political ambitions: "I just want to say a few things to my black brothers, who I know are not going to endorse me. I do not expect their support, nor will I bother them about it. . . . They are the prisoners of their traditional attitudes and some of them are just plain jealous because they have been wounded in their male egos." She told these men to "get off my back, and if I make the race I want it to be clear that it will be without seeking anyone's endorsement." Concluding on a conciliatory note, she still emphasized her support for black women. "Brothers . . . black women are not here to compete or fight with you. If we have hang-ups about being male or female, we're going to waste the talents that should be put to use to liberate our people. Black women must be able to give what they have in the struggle."[14]

On November 18–20, the Congressional Black Caucus hosted a "National Conference of Black Elected Leaders" at the Shoreham Hotel in Washington, DC. More than three hundred attended. The original purpose was to bring state and local elected officials to Washington to discuss common problems and goals, not to discuss a strategy for the presidential election, but the Northlake meeting had already let the cat—the discussion of the possibility of a black presidential candidate—out of the bag. At one panel session, chaired by Missouri congressional representative William Clay, titled "The Development of Black Political Power in the Seventies," the speakers were Percy Sutton; Carl Stokes, the mayor of Cleveland; Barbara Jordan, then Texas state senator; and Howard Lee, the mayor of Chapel Hill, New Jersey. During the question period, Florida state representative Gwendolyn Cherry stood and asked why Chisholm, a possible presidential candidate, was not on the panel.

Cherry, an outspoken feminist, had much in common with Chisholm. The first African American woman to practice law in Dade County and the first African American woman elected to the Florida Legislature (in 1970), she had introduced the Equal Rights Amendment in the legislature in 1972. To stave off a brouhaha that would once again put her not-yet-declared candidacy in the spotlight, Chisholm, who was at the conference, explained that when the meeting had first been organized, no such panel had been proposed and that she herself had volunteered to be on the panel discussing early childhood education. However, she reminded the audience, "I am the highest elected woman official today and for those who don't know, the Democratic National Committeewoman from the State of New York. You better wake up."[15]

Chisholm later said that she would have chosen to participate on a panel on national politics had she been told that there was one. "It seemed to me clear that there had been a subtle, but unmistakable attempt to keep me out of the limelight and there was no possibility that I would ever gain the unified backing of the caucus."[16] A month later, at Cherry's invitation, Chisholm went to Florida to see if she could raise money and support to help her make up her mind about running.

In the end, many factors contributed to Chisholm's decision to run. The drive by the Congressional Black Caucus to find a suitable black candidate was just one. Students' and women's groups constantly pressured her to run. One day in November 1971, Chisholm walked into her office after a speaking tour and announced, "You know, I think I am going to do something no one is going to believe." "What is that?" asked an aide, Carolyn Smith. "I am going to run for

President," Chisholm responded, and Smith shot back, "President of what?" "For your understanding, Mrs. Smith, "Chisholm replied, "I am going to run for the President of the United States."

Chisholm then called in her entire staff to tell them of her intention. Two other major staffers, Shirley Downs and Thad Garrett, "thought she was out of her ever-loving mind." Garrett asked, "Mrs. Chisholm? Do you know the work that's in that? You thought it was hard work running every two years as a member of Congress, and from Brooklyn, and now you are going to run for president? How are we going to get a committee together?"

According to Smith, it was members of the Congressional Black Caucus who were most upset by Chisholm's announcement. Bill Clay asked sarcastically, "Who does she think she is, running for President of the United States. She needs to know where her place is." Smith said that Clay thought it was fine for Chisholm to be a legislator and represent her district. "In other words, tend to your business. It was okay for Jesse Jackson to run, and it's okay for the men to run—but a lady's place was either in the home, the schools, as a teacher." An exception was Ron Dellums, who told her, "Shirley, if you feel this is what you must do in order to open doors for someone else to come behind you then fine. You know you have my support."

Chisholm used the derision of many CBC members to strengthen her resolve: "I will let them know, you know, women can do the job just as well as the men can." Indeed, "out on the Chisholm Trail," Smith recalls, she was able to reach an awful lot of people—white, black, grey—with her brain power and the fact she could articulate."[17]

Thus it was that on January 25, 1972, Shirley Chisholm stood behind the pulpit of Concord Baptist Church in Bedford-Stuyvesant and announced that she was running for the Democratic Party nomination for the presidency of the United States. Smiling and waving, she addressed the cheering crowd of seven hundred and declared, "I am not the candidate of black America, although I am black and proud. I am not the candidate of the women's movement of this country, although I am a woman and am equally proud of that." She also assured her supporters that she was not "the candidate of any political boss or fat cats or special interests."

It was therefore with Chisholm's candidacy already a fait accompli that a culminating black leadership conference was held March 11, 1972, in Gary, Indiana. By all accounts, it was the largest African American political convention in US history. More than twelve thousand attended. Every political tendency in the black movement was there as well as celebrities, journalists, and politicians. The nascent black feminist movement was not represented, although a number of prominent African American women, including Dorothy Height, Florynce Kennedy, Coretta Scott King, poet Nikki Giovanni, civil rights activist Rosa Parks, and Betty Shabazz, widow of Malcolm X and activist in her own right, attended but did not speak. Hannah Diggs Atkins, the first African American woman elected to the Oklahoma Legislature, was one of the three plenary conveners or chairs of the conference, but resigned this position due to what she described as Amiri Baraka's "brutish attacks" on her.

Organized and chaired by the troika of Baraka, Diggs, and Hatcher, the conference, according to Manning Marable, "represented the zenith of black nationalism . . . the entire black movement." Its goal was "to move the black masses from the politics of desegregation to . . . create their own black political party." The document it produced, a draft National Black Political Agenda, was praised by Marable as "the most visionary and progressive statement ever issued by African Americans about their position in this country."[18] Radical Black Nationalism was the dominant theme. As they sang the Black National anthem, "Lift Every Voice and Sing," even pacifists and integrationists like Coretta Scott King and Dorothy Height were raising the radical Black Nationalist gesture of the clenched fist. Swept up in nationalist excitement, delegates chanted the slogan "Nationtime! Nationtime! Nationtime!" Despite all the enthusiasm, however, the Gary convention never came to grips with the difficulties of bridging hierarchies of age, class, gender, sexuality, region, ethnicity, national origin, and politics among African Americans.

Chisholm did not go to the Gary conference. She knew she would not get any support from the organizers, most of whom believed that the first African American to run for president should be a man. Some were still angry that she had decided to run for president without their approval. One political figure told Thomas Johnson of the *New York Times,* "We found out that she was running after we all met in Chicago at a black doctor's house last summer to talk about running a black man for President. We called Shirley to ask her support and she said she was going to run herself." Whether Chisholm actually affirmed her desire to run or not, this comment reflected the concerns raised by black politicians about the impact of the women's movement on the 1972 campaign. "The specter of white women bargaining in the Democratic convention with white men on behalf of the black community was a frightening thing," explained one unnamed black politician.[19] This quote underscores both the gender and the racial dynamics facing black women who were feminists and aspiring political actors. The assumption—strongly held, but not accurate—was that the women's movement was all white and racist and that black women needed to show their support for their men.

Chisholm was criticized then and even forty years later for not attending this important convention. However, there was little reason for her to do so. She did not want to be the center of a debate over whether she should run for president. As far as she was concerned, the issue was moot; she had announced her candidacy two and a half months earlier and was already campaigning. Second, according to Marion Humphrey, an Arkansan from Pine Bluff and a Princeton University student who worked on her presidential campaign, Chisholm did not "want her candidacy to be portrayed simply as a black candidacy at the time." Chisholm saw herself as the candidate of all the people, not one particular constituency.[20] Finally, Chisholm found the rhetoric of some of the Black Nationalist leaders, in particular Amiri Baraka, offensive and misogynistic. Hannah Diggs Atkins had resigned a leadership position in disgust over Baraka's public behavior, and Chisholm, very familiar with this rhetoric, no doubt did not wish to have it surround her. Furthermore, nothing in the conference agenda specifically addressed black women's issues. No women spoke at the plenary.

Chisholm's choice not to go turned out to be justified. Marion Humphrey attended the Gary conference, wearing his Chisholm "Unbought and Unbossed" buttons, only to be greeted with hostile glares. In a crowded elevator, a woman cornered him and said, "Every time I see one of those buttons I get sick." Humphrey did not know what to say: "I am too much of a southerner to be disrespectful to the ladies." But another occupant of the elevator, Chisholm supporter Florynce Kennedy, turned on the woman and retorted, "Then why don't you just throw up?"[21]

In the end, after all the meetings—secret and open—caucuses, and conferences, the Gary conference produced no unified strategy for a black presidential candidate. Chisholm had the support of CBC members Ron Dellums and Parren Mitchell, US congressman from Maryland, and of Percy Sutton. And as she had said, she intended to run regardless of the CBC's lack of endorsement or the outright sexist hostility of much of the black male leadership, for she claimed to have the support of ordinary citizens—black, Latino, women, men, veterans, and youth.

9

On the Chisholm Trail

In her speech at Concord Baptist Church announcing her candidacy for president, Chisholm asked for support from all those she considered her constituents. Most especially, she called upon:

> Those of you who were locked outside of the convention hall in 1968, those of you who can now vote for the first time, those of you who agree with me that the institutions of this country belong to all of the people who inhabit it. Those of you who have been neglected, left out, ignored, forgotten or shunted aside for whatever reason, give me your help at this hour. Join me in an effort to reshape our society and regain control of our destiny as we go down the Chisholm Trail for 1972.[1]

Chisholm's presidential campaign was the high point of her political career. Her intention was to shake up the political system, and she hoped to engage African Americans, women, young people, lesbians and gay men, veterans, the poor, the elderly, Native Americans, Chicanos—the very people who had been marginalized by the political system—in the struggle for a more just society. She was under no illusion that she had a chance of winning the presidency, let alone even the Democratic nomination. She was also politically pragmatic. Along with her hopes of mobilizing large numbers, she ran in the primary campaigns in order to win enough delegate votes and be a political force at the Democratic National Convention. Her campaign did more than, as she put it, "crack a little more of the ice which in recent years has congealed to nearly immobilize our political system": she dared to pry open the door of the privileged white-male-only US presidency. As she wrote in *The Good Fight*, "I ran because somebody had to do it first"—and she was the best person to do it.[2]

Yet all of Chisholm's steely determination, her courage, intellect, self-confidence, and grassroots support, was not enough to win any significant Democratic primary battles. Although she was not, as her staffers had thought, "out of her ever-loving mind," she was out of her league in mounting a campaign for the presidency. The list of challenges was endless. While she was able to run a competent office in Washington, DC, and in Brooklyn, New York, she and her staff were not prepared for the overwhelming demands of a national presidential campaign. Her own inexperience, her lack of a national campaign staff, a dysfunctional and feuding campaign staff in Washington, the lack of serious fund-raising capacity, the campaign's reliance on untrained volunteers as opposed to paid professionals, factionalism between white feminists and black community activists among her supporters, media uninterest, and a general belief from Democratic Party operatives that her campaign was a lost cause plagued her operation throughout.

Although she had steeled herself to expect no support from the leadership of the black movement, she was not politically prepared for the hardball tactics used by the other contenders, in particular the McGovern forces. To her extreme surprise and disappointment, Chisholm learned that enthusiastic crowds and devoted grassroots supporters did not translate into votes at the polls. Even so, she finished the campaign seventh out of a field of seventeen candidates. She also became the first woman to win a Democratic primary, and at the convention in July 1972 she became—and remains—the only woman whose name has been placed into nomination to be the Democratic candidate for president.

One of the many reasons Chisholm decided to throw her hat—or, as Walter Cronkite, the most respected journalist at the time and the *CBS News* evening anchor, patronizingly called it in his prime-time news broadcast, "her bonnet"—into the ring was her conviction that none of the all-white male candidates could speak to the disaffected constituencies of African Americans, the elderly, women, lesbians and gays, veterans, Latinos, Indians, and younger workers. As she noted, it was the same old faces, the same old song and dance.

As a result of reforms enacted after the disastrous 1968 Democratic nominating convention in Chicago, 1972 was the first time that the winner of the Democratic nomination for the US presidency would be determined by the results of primary and caucus campaigns in the states. The primaries and caucuses were staggered between January and June before the Democratic nominating convention that July. These primary elections and caucuses were run by state and local Democratic Party officials. These primaries and caucus elections are characterized as an indirect election: instead of voters directly selecting a particular person running for president, the caucus or primary determines how many delegates each party's national convention will receive from their respective state. These delegates then in turn select their party's presidential nominee.

In all, fifteen people announced their intention of running for the Democratic nomination for the presidency. The initial front runner was Maine senator Edmund Muskie, who had been Hubert Humphrey's vice presidential nominee in 1968. But Muskie all but wrote off the black vote by admitting that for political reasons, he would never choose an African American as a running mate. Then in March 1972, he destroyed his chance at the nomination when he broke down and wept in public after a newspaper published a letter claiming that his wife drank. This letter was later revealed to have been forged, as part of the Nixon campaign's practice of using unethical, illegal "dirty tricks" against its opponents. The letter was the work of political operative Donald Segretti, who was in charge of these operations.

In Chisholm's opinion, Hubert Humphrey, Lyndon Johnson's vice president and the 1968 presidential candidate, was the best of the white male candidates. He was liberal. He had some civil rights credentials and supported Johnson's Great Society. However, because he had been Johnson's veep, he was damaged goods. Humphrey was contaminated by his support for the war in Vietnam and for Chicago's mayor Richard Daley's violent suppression of dissent during the disastrous riots at the 1968 convention. Although Humphrey won the popular vote in the 1972 primaries, he lost the nomination because he did not get enough delegates.

George Wallace, former governor of Alabama, segregationist, and avowed opponent of busing students as a means of integrating the public schools, affirmative action, and radical social protest movements, was, as expected, Chisholm's least favorite candidate. Wallace won the Florida, Michigan, and Maryland primaries. The third major candidate, George McGovern, senator from North Dakota, who wound up winning the nomination, was a liberal who opposed the Vietnam War and was supported by the Kennedys. McGovern's success was based on his strategy of winning primaries through grassroots support despite establishment opposition. He began the campaign with one great advantage: having led a commission to redesign the Democratic nomination system after the disastrous 1968 convention, he knew better than any other candidate that the Democratic primaries would now determine the nominee—not caucuses or party leaders, as in the past. McGovern won eight primaries and collected the most delegates. To Chisholm, despite his liberal politics, he ranked only just above Wallace. She considered McGovern and his campaign staff the worst sort of white elitist liberals, who thought they could speak and act for the black community.

Other candidates who dropped out during the primaries included Washington senator Henry (Scoop) Jackson, who supported the Vietnam War; New York City mayor John Lindsay, a liberal Republican turned Democrat; North Carolina governor Terry Sanford; and Congresswoman Patsy Mink, who appeared only on the Oregon primary ballot. An outspoken opponent of the war, Mink was asked to run in the Oregon primary by a group of women from the Oregon branch of the National Women's Political Caucus. Her campaign was widely publicized in Oregon but virtually unknown elsewhere. She got 5,082 votes in the Oregon primary, 573 votes in Maryland, and 913 votes in Wisconsin, even though she did not campaign in either state.[3]

Chisholm's first test of the difficulties she would face was her foray into the Florida primary. In the past, all her campaigns had been run largely out of her Brooklyn living room. She knew her constituents well; many were school, college, church, and club mates. She was on a first-name basis with the local school administrators, shopkeepers, union leaders, political clubs, bankers, and political operatives. Running a national campaign was a completely different type of operation, and Chisholm had very few national political operatives in her camp. She was invited to run in the Florida primary by Gwen Cherry, who believed she could get support from leaders of both the black and the women's movements in the state. But once arrived in Florida, Chisholm realized that the male black leaders, in particular Florida's Alcee Hastings and Julian Bond, opposed her candidacy. Bond, who had his own presidential ambitions, warned that Chisholm would not win, and worse, "she would embarrass a lot of her own people who have already made commitments to other candidates. She hasn't done her homework and she is simply not known in Florida."[4]

In Florida Chisholm put together a cadre of grassroots volunteers. Remus Allen, a Tallahassee lawyer, and Isaiah Williams, an antipoverty worker from Jacksonville, began handling the details of campaign filings, voter canvassing, and organizing new recruits, most of whom came from college campuses and the civil rights and women's movements. Two young white men, Floridian Roger Barr, an amateur tennis player and coach, and Bob Gottleib, who took a leave of absence from Cornell University to work on the campaign, answered letters; distributed bumper stickers, brochures, and buttons; and organized campaign rallies—all without pay. Both men took a lot of flak from racist whites as well as from some African Americans. Gottleib stayed with the campaign until Miami and regarded working for Chisholm as one of the greatest experiences in his life.

In Florida and elsewhere she was constantly plagued by internecine struggles between the white women in the National Organization for Women and the National Women's Political Caucus and campaign workers from the black community. Both groups demanded her time and attention, and only she could soothe the bruised egos and hurt feelings. Although the white women were tireless workers, devoted to the campaign, and excelled at arranging well-attended meetings and television and newspaper publicity, they did not understand how to connect the issues of abortion, day care, and the Equal Rights Amendment to the concerns of the black civil rights and liberation movements. Furthermore, Chisholm believed that these women were not open to the kind of meaningful coalition politics that her campaign advocated.

A story Chisholm told Jim Pitts, a Massachusetts supporter, about her Florida campaign highlights these conflicts among white and black women. The two groups were fighting over who would take her to the airport. According to Chisholm, the white women insisted, "We are financing this campaign and we are going to take her." The black women retorted, "She's our soul sister and she is going to ride with us!" Annoyed at the squabbling, Chisholm approached a young man nearby and asked if he had a car. He said, "Yeah," and Chisholm got in it, leaving the women still fighting. It is hard to ascertain how accurate this story is, but it does reflect the difficulties white and black women had working together—probably for the first time—in national electoral coalition politics.[5]

Chisholm's Washington office was particularly disorganized. She lost her first and only national campaign manager, Gerald Robinson, after only a month. Robinson left because he found it impossible to put together a statewide campaign organization in Florida out of the confusion of squabbling factions, with no one in the Washington office to back him up. One adviser, Thaddeus Garrett, was at constant loggerheads with Shirley Downs, who was very much tied to the National Women's Political Caucus and their feminist agenda. Garrett, a Republican and not a feminist, was more connected to the Congressional Black Caucus. Liz Cohen, a Princeton undergraduate who worked in the office, witnessed the interaction between the two. "I was fairly baffled about why Thad had the kind of influence that he had because he seemed very cautious and conservative, more so even than Shirley Chisholm herself. I think it's possible that she wanted to balance her advisors because she was a pragmatist; she was no raving radical. She believed in the system, she just wanted to make the system work as well as she could."[6]

Aside from poor management and office dysfunction, the campaign was starved for cash. No professional fund-raisers were on staff. According to a deposition the Chisholm campaign gave in response to a General Accounting Office audit, total contributions totaled $118,620.62, not including the one from Chisholm herself, who made the largest contribution of $32,599.50. The deposition demonstrates the grassroots nature of the campaign; almost half of the contributions came in amounts of $100 and less. Almost $40,000 was raised by organizations.

During the campaign, Chisholm was a member of the House of Representatives with responsibilities in Washington. At the same time, she acted as her own campaign manager. Gerald Robinson considered her campaign "shoddy and poorly organized," likely to lose the support of people who would otherwise have been involved in it. Yet even with this disorganized, unprofessional, and impoverished campaign organization, Chisholm managed to speak at countless schools, colleges, churches, and the Florida State Fair. She marched on picket lines with sugarcane workers, whom she addressed in Spanish. She traveled throughout the state in a chartered bus called the Chisholm Express. Sometimes the campaign's lack of organization meant that she showed up for rallies that had just been canceled or had never been organized. Meetings and press conferences were constantly rescheduled, often without informing the newspapers, radio stations, and meeting organizers. Campaign volunteers (once, a group of schoolchildren) would be dispatched to canvass, but the local office was never informed. Dates and places of meetings were often misspelled, or the wrong addresses were listed. Ruefully, Chisholm reflected that Muskie, Lindsay, and Humphrey had well-paid staffers and traveled in chartered planes, trains, and limousines, while she campaigned in volunteers' cars and slept in their homes.

Another factor that didn't help the campaign was that Chisholm never hesitated to say what she thought on the issues. In Miami, speaking to a group of Cuban Americans, she did not realize that most were upper-class members of prerevolutionary Cuban society, staunchly anticommunist, and aligned with the right wing of the Republican Party. On the other side of the political fence, she startled many liberal Democrats and members of the civil rights community by her opposition to busing, a bitterly disputed court-ordered solution to the problems of school segregation. "Busing is an artificial way of solving the segregation problem," she would say. "Open housing is the real way." But she excoriated whites who opposed busing as hypocrites. "Where were you when for years black children were bused out of their neighborhoods and carried miles on rattle trap buses, down back roads to a dirty school with a tarpaper roof and no toilets? If you believed in neighborhood schools, where were you then?" In contrast to Chisholm's forthrightness, McGovern, Muskie, and Humphrey hemmed and hawed on the issue. At one point, George Wallace commented that Chisholm was the only candidate besides himself who had the same position on busing regardless of constituency or region.[7]

When asked by a group of Florida State University students what she would do to protect the environment, she "let them have it straight," asking, "How can I be worried about the threat to the mammals in the remote oceans? The real environmental problem is in the slums where people live surrounded by garbage and their children eat the peeling chips of lead paint and are bitten by rats. . . . Let's do something about the children first, and then worry about the whales." Finally, speaking on foreign policy to an all-white, all-male luncheon audience at the Tiger Bay Men's Club in Miami—the first time the club had hosted a woman speaker—she stressed that the primary concern of US policy in the Middle East should be the plight of the Palestinian refugees. Audience members attacked her for being pro-Arab, and she was unable to convince them that she was neither pro-Arab nor pro-Israeli, but rather against people's suffering.[8]

Still, there were extraordinary moments. She had the support of two larger than life artists and civil rights activists, Ossie Davis and Harry Belafonte, who appeared at fund-raisers and gave generously to her campaign. As she traveled throughout the state, she often spoke in public places where no African American had ever dared to speak. For example, North Florida was known as "South Georgia" or "real Wallace country." In the panhandle town of Quincy, she was joined by the Reverend Ralph Abernathy of the Southern Christian

Leadership Conference, one of the major civil rights organizations. "A few years ago," he told the crowd of several thousand African Americans and a few whites, "we could not have stood here on the steps of this courthouse and had this kind of rally." Chisholm was overwhelmed that large numbers of elderly African Americans attended her rallies, some raising clenched fists when she began to speak.

Her next stop was the town of Marianna, the site of a much-publicized 1934 lynching and race riot. Marianna had not seen a presidential candidate in twenty years, and on that day two came to speak—Wallace and Chisholm. Understandably, everyone was tense. Chisholm spoke on the steps of the county courthouse. "Nearby, as everywhere in the South, there was a statue of a Confederate soldier. . . . [T]he rifle the statue was holding seemed almost to be pointing at me," Chisholm remembered. An elderly black man approached her, saying, "I never thought I'd live to see a black person speaking from the court house steps."[9] Wallace followed later in the day. The national press ignored Chisholm but covered Wallace, who won the primary with 42 percent of the vote. Chisholm received 3 percent.

Even with a poorer showing than she had hoped for, and despite being plagued by lack of money and her staff's disorganization, Chisholm continued her campaign undaunted, with a growing number of dedicated grassroots volunteers. Among them was a young Al Sharpton, civil rights activist and today host of MSNBC's *PoliticsNation,* who headed her New York City Youth for Chisholm operation. Jill Franklin, a white radical student activist from New York, wrote her speech on women's rights. Victor Robles was one of Chisholm's staunchest supporters and hardest campaign workers. He had grown up in Williamsburg, Brooklyn, the son of the Puerto Rican American community activist Aurea M. Blanco. After the 1972 campaign, Robles continued to work on Chisholm's staff and was instrumental in helping with her Brooklyn Puerto Rican constituents. Chisholm and Robles were devoted to each other. Basil Paterson commented that Chisholm treated Robles as the son she wished she had. He later became the New York State assemblyman from the Fifty-Third District. From 1982 to 2001, he served as a New York City councillor, championing among many issues, marriage equality.

Other prominent individuals and organizations who supported Chisholm included civil rights activist Rosa Parks, NOW president Wilma Scott Heide, Republican psychologist and board member of the National Women's Political Caucus JoAnn Evansgardner, NAACP activist Alma Fox, Mississippi Freedom Democratic Party leader and civil rights activist Fannie Lou Hamer, and United Farm Workers' Union organizer and activist Lupe Anguiano. Gloria Steinem and Betty Friedan unsuccessfully ran as Chisholm delegates to the Democratic National Convention from New York State. New York supporters who were elected as Chisholm delegates all were or became important New York City political figures, including Florynce Kennedy; Carl McCall, first African American comptroller of New York State and the 2002 Democratic candidate for governor; and Paul O'Dwyer, a liberal civil rights and anti-war activist, twice elected to the New York City Council.

For Chisholm, the support she got from mainstream feminists was problematic. Many offered only lukewarm support, either because they had their own political ambitions or because they assumed a Chisholm victory was impossible. Bella Abzug, one of the most prominent feminists in Congress, was present at Chisholm's second announcement of her candidacy, this one in Washington, DC, a few days after her Brooklyn announcement, but would not endorse her. All Abzug would say was that Chisholm's campaign was "an idea whose time has come." Steinem qualified her political support. She ran as a Chisholm delegate in the New York State primary, but had stated publicly, "I'm for Shirley Chisholm—but I think George McGovern is the best of the *male* candidates." This ambivalence began to exasperate Chisholm, until she confronted Steinem on a Chicago television program. "Gloria, you're supporting either George McGovern or Shirley Chisholm. I don't mind if you are supporting George. If he is your candidate, so be it, but don't do me any favors by giving me this semi-endorsement. I don't need this kind of help."[10] Thirty-eight years later, at a tribute to Chisholm at Brooklyn College, Steinem expressed regret that she had never sought Chisholm out to explain her position and heal the rift.

By contrast, women of color, having been "long active in civil rights movements and other minority causes, were used to taking up seemingly impossible challenges," Chisholm wrote. Although they might not win their immediate objective, "they would make some gains and in the process increase the chance that success would come someday." She noted that the only times when white and black women worked together were when women of color who had been active in both the civil rights and the women's movements were on hand.

The conflicts between white feminists and activists in the black community continued to plague the campaign through the California primary in June. The continued lack of professional financial and political operatives exacerbated this factionalism, and although Chisholm understood why this conflict existed, she did not have the resources to resolve it.

Chisholm also had to deal with a sometimes hostile media, which—when it covered her campaign at all—was chauvinistic and often patronizing in a manner never shown toward any of the men running for office. The media constantly referred to her small size and used terms never applied to men—*feisty, pepper pot,* or *prim,* to name just a few. Flo Kennedy remarked that Chisholm was "not blacked out or blocked out, she was whited out." This was nothing new, but it was still infuriating. Still, she fought back. A Chisholm supporter filed a protest with the Federal Communications Commission after Chisholm was ignored by the three major news networks (ABC, CBS, and NBC) and excluded from the Sunday morning press shows. At first the networks and the FCC claimed to be exempt from any equal opportunity rule, and the case went to the US Court of Appeals. Within hours the FCC reversed its ruling and ordered all three networks to provide Chisholm with one half hour of prime airtime. She asked Gloria Steinem to help write the speech she would give on television. Steinem recalled, "The still unmatched moment of pride in my life was that she asked me to write it. Of course it was always her message and it was only my listening to her speech that made me able to do it. Nonetheless I'll never forget watching television hearing Shirley speak words that I had worked so hard to make worthy of her and of the historic occasion."[11]

Unlike McGovern, Humphrey, or Wallace, Chisholm did not have a coherent, well-mapped-out plan for the Democratic primaries. She chose to run in some primaries, like Florida, for example, because she thought she had enough supporters to create an effective campaign. In other cases, she entered a primary after supporters entered her without her knowledge. Time, money, and the capacity of her campaign staff dictated her primary sources. Chisholm wanted to enter the Washington, DC, primary. She was very popular in DC and even expected to win. Furthermore, campaigning there would not be that difficult or expensive, for she could tend to her congressional duties during the primary campaign. But she could not run in that primary, because Walter Fauntroy intended to run in DC as a "favorite son" (a candidate from a particular locality). However, he promised to release his delegates to her on the second ballot at the convention. Chisholm was skeptical, but had to go along. She also ran in New Jersey, where she campaigned in all thirteen counties, an effort coordinated by Princeton student Marion Humphrey, and won the primary in that state by 67 percent. This was a "preference" primary, or "beauty contest," as it was called, because the vote was nonbinding. Consequently, this victory did not translate into delegate votes.

The different sets of rules and procedures for electing delegates among the states were an added complication of the primary race because the McGovern commission rules allowed each state to develop its own primary procedures, provided they follow the overall commission guidelines. Amid all the political complexities, grassroots activists rose to the challenge. Jo Freeman, feminist, political scientist, author, and activist, was a graduate student at the University of Chicago when she joined Chisholm's campaign in March 1972. She understood immediately that the first thing to do was get Chisholm's name on the ballot for the Illinois primary in March, a week after the Florida primary. This was no easy task. Largely due to her dislike of Chicago mayor Richard Daley's political machine, which controlled the city's Democratic Party, Freeman was not involved in Chicago politics. Illinois did not have a preference primary. Instead, individuals ran for election as delegates to the Democratic National Convention from each congressional district. They could either commit themselves to a specific candidate or run uncommitted. Only presidential candidates who had committed delegates running in a given district appeared on that district's ballot, so Freeman needed to get herself on the ballot in her home district in Hyde Park as a delegate committed to Chisholm.

Aware that the Daley machine would run its own slate of delegate candidates, Freeman looked elsewhere for support. She did not get much from Chicago's black leadership. When she approached Operation PUSH, headed by the Reverend Jesse Jackson, for help getting on the ballot, she was treated with mild disdain. But with support from University of Chicago graduate students, she collected enough signatures to appear on the primary ballot, committed to Chisholm. The local Chicago campaign wrote Chisholm's office, letting her know she would be on the ballot. Immediately, they received one hundred buttons, twenty bumper stickers, and nine position papers on foreign affairs. Grassroots volunteers received no other support from Chisholm's campaign office, so they did all the local campaigning, including arranging meetings, canvassing, posting notices, and sending out local press releases about Chisholm and the election. It was difficult to find a free venue for Chisholm to speak in Chicago, so she made only one appearance there, at Malcolm X Junior College. Jackson would not invite Chisholm to speak at the Operation PUSH building.

As expected, the Daley machine won all eight delegate slots in the First District. Freeman came in ninth in a field of twenty-four, beating people committed to George McGovern and Edward M. Kennedy (who did not run, but was very popular). Immediately after the election, the McGovern forces successfully challenged the Daley delegation, which had made no attempt to comply with new party guidelines requiring that delegations reflect the composition of their districts by race, sex, and age. Freeman supported the legal challenge and became a Chisholm alternate to the Miami convention.[12]

In some states, Chisholm won votes with only one visit. In New Mexico, Tashia Young, a thirty-seven-year-old mother of five, asked permission to put Chisholm's name on the ballot. With five hundred dollars she had borrowed, she organized campaign offices in Albuquerque, Las Cruces, and Farmington. In Pittsburgh the local NOW chapter held a Chisholm rally that attracted a standing-room-only crowd of more than five thousand people. Eleanor Smeal, today president of the Feminist Majority Foundation, was a NOW activist there. "As a young feminist leader in Pittsburgh, her speeches were inspiring," Smeal recalled.

Sometimes, though, the campaign had to make wrenching, difficult decisions that disillusioned Chisholm's supporters. Liz Cohen, a campaign organizer in Wisconsin, described an "upsetting, sobering situation for me, a learning situation." The Washington office was contacted by people in Madison connected to the University of Wisconsin and by a minister in nearby Racine who wanted to mount a primary campaign. Cohen and Bob Gottlieb went to Wisconsin, stayed in people's homes, and began planning for a Chisholm visit. "I was so impressed with these people; they had no resources from us. They were raising the pennies they had to run this campaign; they were planning events for when she came," Cohen recalled. At the last minute, Chisholm's office told Cohen that Chisholm was not coming to Wisconsin. Cohen was shocked. The staff person explained, "At this point, if she goes, she would only be there two or three days, she wouldn't probably do that well. If she doesn't step into the state, then we can say she got 5% of the vote and she didn't even campaign there. If she goes there, then people will say she campaigned and only got 5% of the vote." Dumbstruck, Cohen protested, "But these people out there, they are working so hard. They have been working for weeks, months; they think she's coming. We can't let them down." The response was, "That's politics—she's not going." Cohen then had to call everyone with the disappointing news. Furious, the Wisconsin supporters cried, "How could you do that? Isn't the whole point of this campaign to mobilize people for good causes? To keep progressive politics alive on a local level? This is not really about winning—how could she let us down like this?"

For Cohen, this incident illustrated a central contradiction of the campaign—how to reconcile the idealism of Chisholm's grassroots supporters with the difficult realities of political campaigns. On the one hand, local supporters wanted to use the Chisholm campaign to empower people and give them some sort of ammunition for their own local coalitions. On the other, Chisholm wanted to win, and she cared about her reputation. "These objectives collided and that Wisconsin story is an example of where it collided. And it was very hard for me to accept and it made it a lot harder to give hope and encouragement to people out in the field, when I knew we might let them down."[13]

Chisholm entered the Massachusetts primary after two supporters, Jim Pitts and Saundra Graham, called and told her that if she came to Massachusetts, they would help organize her campaign. Pitts, a liberal antiwar African American Democrat, had read *Unbought and Unbossed* at the beginning of the primary season. Pitts and Graham, a Cambridge councilwoman, contacted Mark Solomon, a Brooklyn-born professor at Simmons College in Boston, and the three began to organize. They started with a meeting of the Worcester Caucus of Progressive Democrats, where Solomon made a successful case for supporting Chisholm. Massachusetts, he insisted, had to send an "indisputable message, an unambiguous message about peace, and about racial equality, about the struggles for civil rights and for women's rights." Afterward, a man from Watertown approached Solomon and told him, "Hey, I changed my vote—I was going to vote for McGovern, but this argument about sending the strongest possible message to the Democrats in the first place, and to the country in general, is a strong message."[14]

Chisholm went to Massachusetts more than a dozen times, speaking mainly at college campuses. Solomon recalled that the Simmons College president was so thrilled to have her speak that he built a large podium in the quad, put up flags and banners, and made remarks himself as Solomon introduced Chisholm. Some of the meetings were not very successful. One of Chisholm's biggest backers was supposed to host a large fund-raiser at her Boston mansion. The problem was that this woman was married to a vice president of Polaroid, a company that not only supported South African apartheid, but had just fired a group of employees who belonged to the prodivestment Polaroid Revolutionary Movement. One PRM member was a leading Chisholm supporter. A huge debate ensued about whether to hold the meeting in the Polaroid executive's home. Pitts had to call Chisholm for advice, pulling her off the floor of Congress. Without hesitation she said they must change the venue. They did, and the executive's wife attended, bringing friends. Pitts laughed ruefully about that experience. "It was a good lesson for me about how coalition politics is really difficult, and you can't always have it the right way, the way you want it." Asked how Chisholm described coalition politics, Pitts laughed again and said, "It was a bitch."[15]

At another fund-raiser, Solomon, a Chisholm delegate, promised that if the candidate won enough primary delegates, the Chisholm forces could "play a power broker role" at the Miami convention. "She is a dark horse in a grey field of white male candidates," adding, "She's the only candidate I'd accept a kiss from," an introduction Chisholm particularly loved.[16]

Chisholm spoke not only in wealthy neighborhoods, but also at black colleges, in the African American neighborhood of Roxbury, and to a Latino audience at Cardinal Cushing High School in Boston. At one Sunday afternoon rally at the Charles Street African Methodist Episcopal Church, several young members of the gay liberation movement walked noisily down the aisles, wearing colorful, striking costumes. (Chisholm, always a fashionista, wrote that one man's cape was beautiful: "I wanted it.") The young men, to the shocked looks of the older African American parishioners, waved their hands, shouting, "Hiya Shirley! Right on, gal!" Chisholm, who had already declared her support for homosexual rights and equality, was delighted to have their support, "although I only wish they were not camping it up quite so flagrantly," she wrote at the time.[17] The gay men ended up handing out flyers for her.

This anecdote shows how Chisholm relished the challenges of coalition politics. She believed in it and worked hard to bring what may seem very disparate elements together—especially groups whose civil rights had been infringed upon and those who had been marginalized by society. One feature of Chisholm's Massachusetts campaign was its diversity in terms of age, class, ethnicity, gender, race, and sexuality. It included many young people from community colleges as well as from Harvard. There were older, more established radical grassroots political figures such as Mel King, who later ran for mayor of Boston; Hubie Jones, who became dean of social work at Boston University; and Steve Curwood, an established journalist who regularly appeared on local public radio.[18] Both the Chisholm and McGovern campaigners in the state were progressive Democrats, committed to serious coalition politics, which they continued past the 1972 election. Jim Pitts pointed out that Massachusetts was the only state that did not go for Nixon in 1972 and credits, in part, the coalition work of the Chisholm-McGovern forces. Chisholm came in fifth in Massachusetts, with 22,398 votes. But she also won seven delegates. One, Jim Pitts, was elected to the party's Platform Committee, and Saundra Graham, also a delegate, served on the important Credentials Committee.

In Ann Arbor, Michigan, an African American pharmacist named Jacqui Hoop joined with a white political activist, Becky O'Malley, to organize the Chisholm for President Headquarters. The Michigan group consisted largely of women who had been working since the early 1960s to end various forms of discrimination and, after 1964, to end the war in Vietnam. They were not student protesters or counterculturalists but liberal working mothers who raised money through jazz concerts and garage sales and handed out handwritten, mimeographed press releases and flyers on the University of Michigan campus.

Although Chisholm did not win any endorsements from leading Michigan politicians, she won the support of Jane Hart, wife of Democratic senator Phil Hart, who became a major fund-raiser. Support for Chisholm's candidacy grew as it appeared that Wallace would win the white vote in Michigan. Soon campaign offices appeared in Flint, Kalamazoo, East Lansing, Detroit, and Grand Rapids. Chisholm made several trips to Michigan. In her speeches, she constantly referred to the role of black women in the struggle for social justice. "Who knows it took a little black woman, Harriet Tubman, to lead three hundred of her people out of slavery; it required another little black woman, Rosa Parks, to say she was tired of going to the back of the bus." Referring to herself, she ended by saying, "It may take another little black woman to 'bring us together' in these troubled times of war and worry."[19] Always mindful of the history of black women's struggles, she found time in the midst of campaigning in

Battle Creek to lay a wreath on the grave of another black woman, Sojourner Truth, nineteenth-century antislavery activist, lecturer, preacher, and champion of women's rights.

Despite the crowds who came to hear her speak—to say nothing of her stature as a member of Congress—the state party snubbed her. Concerned about Wallace's popularity, the party convened a meeting with representatives from the Muskie, McGovern, and Humphrey campaigns but did not invite Chisholm due to what it called an "oversight." Her presence in Michigan put pressure on Detroit representative John Conyers, a leading member of the CBC. Like most other CBC members, Conyers was not particularly supportive of her campaign and did not want to alienate the Democratic Party leadership. However, Chisholm had a large following in Detroit. So, like Gloria Steinem, he kept his foot in both camps by promising to endorse her in primaries in which McGovern was not running. "I suppose I should have been grateful even for this ambivalent stand," she wrote.[20] Just before the Michigan primary vote, Chisholm made a three-day swing through the state that included speaking at a peace and justice rally before several thousand in Detroit. The next day, she heard from a sheriff's deputy that George Wallace had been shot.

Wallace had won the Florida primary and was a serious contender in the primary race. Then, on May 15, 1972, he was shot five times by Arthur Bremer while campaigning in Laurel, Maryland. He was hit in the abdomen and chest, and because one of the bullets lodged in Wallace's spine he was left paralyzed from the waist down. Every one of the male Democratic Primary contenders visited Wallace in the hospital. But when Chisholm visited him, she was barraged with criticism from many in the African American community—criticism that no white male candidate received. Chisholm was surprised at the excessive press attention and remarked that she got more media attention from her visit to Wallace than almost anything else she did on the campaign trail. Despite their ideological differences and opposition from her supporters, Chisholm felt that visiting Wallace was the humane thing to do. Wallace, in tears, asked with disbelief, "Is that really you Shirley? Have you come to see me?" Chisholm soothingly answered, "You and I don't agree, but you've been shot, and I might be shot, and we are both children of American democracy, so I wanted to come and see you."[21] After her visit, the two continued to have a respectful political relationship. Jim Pitts, who dealt with Wallace and his delegates at the Miami convention, remarked that Wallace had much admiration for Chisholm. He appreciated that she spoke her mind and did not try to water down her strong political positions. In later years, he helped her round up southern white votes for many of her legislative endeavors.

After the shooting, Wallace won the Michigan and Maryland primaries, but his near assassination effectively ended his campaign and his political career. One result of the assassination attempt was round-the-clock Secret Service protection for all candidates. Conrad Chisholm, who served as an unofficial bodyguard for his wife, was particularly relieved, for there had been three confirmed assassination threats made against his wife. Secret Service protection eased his workload.

Along with everything Chisholm had to deal with, the back-and-forth of campaigning and legislating, raising money, managing an overworked and amateur campaign staff, media indifference, and outright hostility by many black male political leaders, she also faced another assault—this time, no doubt, from the Republican Party. On the eve of the final primary campaign, in California, the FBI alerted Chisholm that she had been a victim of a smear campaign. This was doubtless part of Richard Nixon's "dirty tricks" campaign strategy. But what happened to Chisholm was more than a trick. It was an execrable attack that demonstrated the depths of Nixon's and Segretti's moral corruption. Nor was any male Democratic candidate or "enemy" of Nixon ever subjected to such a disgusting scatological smear.

In early June, someone broke into one of Humphrey's campaign headquarters, stole letterhead stationery, and wrote an ungrammatical, poorly spelled press release claiming that Chisholm had been committed to a private home for the mentally ill, that she was a transvestite, and that she was hostile and aggressive to the people she met. It said her physician had written that Chisholm "makes facial grimaces, talks and gesters [sic] to herself, exhibits inexplicable laughter and weeping, and at times has an abnormal interest in urine and feces which she smears on walls and herself." The letter concluded, "The voters of the nation should be aware of candidates [*sic*] full record and background so an intelligent and meaningful choice can be made. Black voters should be made aware of these facts as her strongest appeal is to them." According to later FBI investigations, this bogus press release was sent to a number of black publications. Given the atrocious spelling and grammar, one can only assume that serious organizations and news outlets knew immediately that the charges were false and immediately alerted the FBI. An appalled Humphrey denied having anything to do with the press release, and the FBI subsequently absolved him of any involvement.[22]

Chisholm never mentioned this smear in *The Good Fight*, nor did filmmakers and writers who chronicled the 1972 Democratic primary. Perhaps it was too hateful an incident for even Chisholm to acknowledge. Perhaps if she had acknowledged it, it would only have encouraged even more racial and gendered attacks on her. A few years later, during the Watergate investigations, special prosecutor Archibald Cox took up the case, but the culprits were never identified.

Although Chisholm was somewhat discouraged by her disappointing showing in Michigan (she came in eighth with just 3 percent of the vote), she decided to campaign in California so as not to disappoint her supporters. She had the support of the California National Organization for Women and the California National Women's Political Caucus along with countless unnamed grassroots women's liberation organizations. Barbara Lee was a single mother, a student at Mills College, and on public assistance when she went to work on Chisholm's campaign. Before she did any work, Lee remembers, Chisholm asked if she had registered to vote. That was the beginning of Lee's political journey, and today she is a member of the US House of Representatives.

Pamela Martinez was another grassroots volunteer. Like Lee, she was a single mother and also the first woman of color elected president of the student body at Oakland's Merritt Community College. She went with a group of supporters to a statewide Democratic convention of student leaders. The purpose of the meeting was to involve student activists in Democratic Party electoral activities. She, too, was inspired by Chisholm in part because she had read about Chisholm's commitment to child care. "So my little group and I decided it had to be Shirley Chisholm. When we got there the number one thing that we found out was there weren't a lot of women who were heads of student councils at these junior colleges, community colleges. And there certainly weren't a whole lot of people of color."[23] Martinez campaigned for Chisholm, continuing her activism as a labor organizer. Today she is retired from the executive board of the California health care union United Health Care Workers West.

Chisholm still had problems getting endorsements from black men. Willie Brown, a strong McGovern supporter, did all he could to prevent black Democrats from getting involved in her campaign. She did get support from the Black Panther Party, which by then had eschewed much of its confrontational politics and was creating community service organizations. No doubt, Chisholm enjoyed the irony of winning an endorsement from an organization that more than any other epitomized militant black masculinism. Understanding—though not agreeing with—their earlier calls for armed struggle, Chisholm pointed out that this endorsement was a sign of hope that these young women and men were beginning to understand that in order to change the system, one had to work within it. She was also pleased because the endorsement meant that "the Panthers had succeeded in rising above sex, something that many blacks find difficult; they were supporting me because of my positions and my programs, without regard to my being female."[24]

McGovern won California with 1,550,000 votes; Humphrey got 1,375,000, and Chisholm came in third with 157,435 votes. California's Democratic Party primary had a winner-take-all system, which meant that the winner of the primary won all of the state's delegates to the Democratic nominating convention. California's primary process was one of eight states that violated the McGovern commission rules, and it became a burning issue at the convention in Miami. After six months of campaigning in eleven primaries, shaking hundreds of thousands of hands, answering thousands of questions, dealing with an indifferent and sometimes hostile press, confronting many logistical problems, facing enthusiastic and adoring crowds, and speaking at countless rallies, caucuses, schools, colleges, churches, and community centers, Chisholm was ready to fight for her share of delegates and play a role in shaping the 1972 presidential race. She was ready for Miami.

The Miami convention, like past and present conventions, was designed to be part spectacle and part political rally, spotlighting the presidential and vice presidential candidates, as well as showcasing party leaders and up-and-coming stars. Delegates attend to take care of Democratic Party business and to enjoy a big party. The 1972 convention was not as disastrous as the 1968 debacle in Chicago, but it came close. As a result of the chaos and bloodshed of Chicago, Democratic Party leaders had set up the McGovern-Fraser Commission to come up with reforms that would bring new forces—youth, African Americans, Latinos, Asians, Native Americans, homosexuals, and women—into the party structure. Delegations to party conventions now had to be more inclusive. In particular, there had to be greater representation of women and of racial and ethnic minorities.

The 1972 Miami convention was different from previous conventions in that the McGovern rules succeeded in bringing in the Democratic Party's grassroots base. For some, it looked as though, four years after the Chicago riots, the protesters had become delegates, in charge of the Democratic platform. By all accounts, the convention was exhilarating, exhausting, and fraught with political intrigue: factional infighting, lobbying, and backroom deal making. Celebrities added to the excitement, including actors Warren Beatty and his sister, Shirley MacLaine; feminist icon Gloria Steinem; journalists including feminist Germaine Greer and Hunter S. Thompson of *Rolling Stone;* and novelist Norman Mailer.

The convention was also defined by the presence of grassroots delegates. Rhoda Jacobs from Brooklyn was an example of a McGovern Rules delegate. A political novice, newly married, and right out of college, she came as a McGovern delegate to the convention. Amid all the politicking, she became a Chisholm supporter. Today Jacobs is a member of the New York State Assembly, representing central Brooklyn. Jim Pitts was another McGovern Rules delegate—young, African American, and a political outsider. His Massachusetts delegation elected him over John Kenneth Galbraith, the renowned economist and former ambassador to India under John F. Kennedy. Pitts believed he had won because "they trusted me that the primary thing was to be against that illegal and immoral war."

Pitts described the convention as chaotic. "Everyone had so much to do. Everyone had a caucus." He was in the Youth Caucus, the Black Caucus, and the Massachusetts Caucus as well as on the Platform Committee. Pitts also chaired the Subcommittee on Law, Crime, and Justice. His accomplishments at the 1972 convention demonstrated the truth of Chisholm's belief that delegate strength brought political power. After his committee on law and justice had wrestled with crime, drugs, and gun control, all very complicated, divisive issues, Pitts was successful in getting the Democratic Party platform to call for the abolition of capital punishment. "It was the first and only time in American history that I know of that the call for the abolition of capital punishment was in the Platform of a national campaign."[25]

Before the convention got down to nominating the presidential and vice presidential candidates, two important committees had to meet and deliberate. The Credentials Committee's function was to ensure that every delegate was legally entitled to participate, while the Platform Committee drew up the party's political manifesto.

The first fight took place over the seating of delegates, an issue of great concern to Chisholm. In order to be seated, every delegate had to be approved by the party's Credentials Committee. By July she had no illusions that she could win the nomination, but she wanted as much delegate strength as possible so that she could be a player at the convention. She came in with 28 and sought to capture more at the convention. This quest was not completely successful. Not surprisingly, Walter Fauntroy did not live up to his promise to release the Washington, DC, delegates to Chisholm; he gave them to McGovern. That's what happens "when a preacher gets involved in politics," Chisholm sighed. "He becomes just another politician." She did pick up 23 delegates from Ohio, 21 from Louisiana, 12 from Mississippi, 9 from Pennsylvania, and 2 from Florida, all African Americans. Fauntroy, Stokes, and Clay had promised the 96 Black Caucus delegates to McGovern, but that maneuver backfired. Many of those delegates had never been asked whether they would support

McGovern; others were furious because they questioned McGovern's commitment to the issues outlined at the Gary conference. Still others were shocked at how the CBC leaders treated Chisholm. For example, Congressman William Clay went so far as to publicly question her sanity. Chisholm went to the convention's Black Caucus meeting, pleading with them to vote for her at least on the first ballot. In the end, the caucus voted to endorse Chisholm. But it was too late. Their endorsement came just hours before the roll call vote and after McGovern had locked up the nomination.

There were countless challenges to state delegations. For example, the Illinois delegation, controlled by Chicago mayor Richard Daley, did not conform to the rules and faced seating and voting challenges from the Credentials Committee. But the most dramatic fight was against California's winner-take-all policy. Even though McGovern had won the California primary by only a 5 percent electoral margin, he won all 271 of its delegates. The Chisholm and Humphrey forces argued for a proportional distribution of the delegates among the candidates, which had been one of the McGovern Commission recommendations. Interestingly, McGovern, who led the reform commission, was trying to benefit from his failure to abide by his own rules and not follow them at the convention. Willie Brown, one of California's most charismatic, ambitious, and effective Democratic leaders, promised the McGovern forces he would win the convention over supporting California's winner-take-all primary. Brown tore up the convention floor with an over-the-top speech demanding that he control who was seated as a delegate. Invoking past civil rights martyrs, struggles, and triumphs, he cried out, "Seat my delegation. I did it for you in Mississippi in '64, in Georgia in '68, and now it's California in '72. I desire no less." Raising his voice and pounding on the podium, he demanded, "GIVE ME BACK MY DELEGATION!" The convention went wild in support of Brown. Brown kept his promise: the McGovern delegation was seated, giving McGovern enough votes to clinch the nomination.[26]

Firestorms also broke out over platform issues. Because there was no unanimity about the platform, delegates came prepared to debate and fight for their planks on abortion, homosexual rights, black liberation, the antiwar movement, the death penalty, welfare rights, health care, education, and the role of the police and the armed forces. Many delegates, like Jim Pitts, were attending their first political convention; they saw themselves as a force in history.

Support for abortion and homosexual rights, emotional and divisive issues today, were hotly debated in 1972. Humphrey, McGovern, and Chisholm had all claimed to support a "gay rights" plank. Gay-rights delegates demanded that such a plank be included in the platform, to no avail. For feminists, the most bitter, disappointing defeat was over a plank affirming a woman's right to abortion. McGovern ultimately excised the abortion issue from the platform. In 1972 McGovern was not committed to a woman's right to abortion and tried throughout the primary season to avoid the topic. Steinem and Abzug tried to convince him, but he remained noncommittal. During the platform debates, McGovern claimed that he would let each delegate vote his or her conscience. In reality, the McGovern strategists believed that an abortion plank "would kill George if it got in," and McGovern delegates were instructed to vote against any such support for abortion rights.

McGovern was deeply conflicted over the issue. McGovern delegate, actress, and activist Shirley MacLaine, who supported abortion rights, urged the delegates to vote against the plank. Gloria Steinem organized the feminist delegates, meeting at the Betsy Ross Hotel, to fight for the plank. Three delegates spoke on the issue of abortion: one male right-to-life proponent spoke against, and MacLaine was the second opposition speaker, arguing that although abortion was a fundamental right, it didn't belong in the platform. Steinem, Abzug, and the other feminists were furious; they felt they had been betrayed.

Chisholm was philosophical about this defeat. "Like the blacks, the women had failed to get it together at Miami; too many had made commitments to a candidate ahead of time and their adherence to him made it impossible for them to work effectively for the cause." Her criticism was searing: "Women like Shirley MacLaine and blacks like Willie Brown were the targets of accusations that they had sold out to McGovern. It seems to me that 'sold out' is the wrong interpretation; they were not bought. They gave themselves away."[27]

But the biggest, bitterest, most heartwrenching disappointment for Chisholm came just hours before her name was to be placed in nomination. Ron Dellums, her one friend and ally in the CBC, who had supported her campaign from its inception and promised to give the speech nominating her, backed out at the last minute. For the previous six months, Willie Brown had worked relentlessly to convince him not to support Chisholm. As the convention approached, the McGovern forces increased the pressure, and in the end he decided his political future was better served by endorsing McGovern. Chisholm was heartbroken. During the campaign, she had experienced endless disappointments, political and personal attacks, snubs, and sexist behavior. But this rejection came from a colleague and friend. In retrospect, looking at who it was that led the attacks on Chisholm and failed to live up to their promises—all African American men: Jackson, Bond, Clay, Fauntroy, Baraka, Brown, and then Dellums—it becomes clear why Chisholm said repeatedly that she experienced more discrimination "as a woman than as a black."

Chisholm was officially nominated on Wednesday night, July 12, by her friend and ally Percy Sutton. In an impassioned speech, he told the crowd, "If my mouth dries up on me, if my tongue becomes large in my mouth, if my voice becomes quavery, if by my appearance I am nervous, please know that I am. I am tense. I am nervous, and I am excited." Reminding the audience of the black struggle, invoking Emmett Till, Medgar Evers, Malcolm X, Martin Luther King Jr., and the murdered civil rights workers Chaney, Schwerner, and Goodman, Sutton presented Chisholm as the embodiment of the heroism of the past and the only person with the integrity, determination, compassion, and understanding to summon "each of us to march towards change, to bring out the best in ourselves—to overcome our racial fears and differences. . . . This candidate has given a voice to the voiceless. She has brought hope to the hopeless."[28] Charles Evers, brother of murdered civil rights leader Medgar Evers and mayor of Fayette, Mississippi, seconded the nomination.

There was one moment of humor in this for Jim Pitts, who recalls that he was elected by the Massachusetts delegation to announce that his state was awarding all its delegate votes to George

McGovern. But he couldn't do it. He told the McGovern delegates that there was no way—he could not vote for McGovern. The Mc-Govern delegates reminded him that he was legally bound, by state and convention rules, to abide by the decision of the majority. So when the moment came to announce the Massachusetts delegate vote, Pitts was nowhere to be found. He had fled to the men's room to keep his conscience clear.

The chaos of the convention did not end with McGovern winning the delegate vote. At three the next morning, George McGovern "won the most worthless presidential nomination of all time," as James Richardson, Willie Brown's biographer, put it. McGovern gave the all-important acceptance speech at an hour when no one, not even the press, was up.[29] On the last night of the convention, in a display of party unity, Chisholm appeared on the dais to a wildly enthusiastic ten-minute ovation. Basil Paterson corralled two New York State delegates, a young Hazel Dukes (now president of the New York City NAACP) and community activist Mary Pickett, to join Chisholm on the platform in a show of sisterly support. Chisholm had not prepared a speech, but she remembered crying out, "Brothers and sisters! At least, I've reached this spot!" As she looked out on the crowd, she was struck by the number of older African American women and men, many with tears in their eyes, others with faces full of joy. "I thought I could read their lives' experiences in their faces at that instant, and I knew what it was they felt. For a moment they really believed it: 'We have overcome.'"[30] Chisholm promised the cheering delegates that she would be an enthusiastic campaigner for George McGovern. And then she left the national stage.

However, the McGovern forces were slow to include Chisholm in the presidential campaign. They set up a "Blacks for McGovern" committee, but never included her in it. She was convinced that the African American men McGovern consulted—Walter Fauntroy, Jesse Jackson, Julian Bond, and Louis Stokes—advised his staff to ignore her. Finally, they asked her to do some campaigning for McGovern in Brooklyn and then in Pennsylvania. She spoke at a rally of four thousand at Lincoln University, a historically black college, and then in Philadelphia.

Ultimately, Nixon won the election in one of the largest landslides in US history. He received almost 18 million more popular votes than McGovern and won every state except Massachusetts and the District of Columbia. Although Chisholm was very critical of the way McGovern had run his campaign, she got no satisfaction from his defeat. Nixon's reelection did not bode well for the future of the urban liberal politics she espoused. Reflecting on her campaign, she pointed out that if she ever decided to mount another presidential run, better planning, a professional paid staff, more effective coalition building, and, of course, better fund-raising would all be essential. *The Good Fight* contains her critique of black politicians, the McGovern machine, and her own campaign mistakes.

Chisholm never regretted her presidential run. "I ran because somebody had to do it first. In this country everybody is supposed to be able to run for President, but that's never been really true. I ran *because* most people think the country is not ready for a black candidate, not ready for a woman candidate. Someday. . . . "[31]

10

Political and Personal Transformations

Although McGovern lost in one of the most lopsided landslides in presidential history, his electoral rout had little impact on Chisholm's reelection. She won with more than 87 percent of the vote and served in Congress for another decade. She was now no longer a junior member who had to fight to be recognized. Her presidential campaign had increased her national visibility and popularity. A 1974 Gallup Poll listed her as one of the top-ten most admired women in America—tied with Indian prime minister Indira Gandhi for sixth place and ahead of Jacqueline Kennedy Onassis and Coretta Scott King. She had no intention of running again for the presidency, but instead became a more conventional politician, using her position in Washington to influence national legislation as well as to consolidate her power in Brooklyn, through bringing home more money and projects for her constituents.

Almost immediately after the election, the Nixon administration began an audit of Chisholm's campaign, charging her with mishandling three contributions totaling $686. Chisholm believed that the investigation was purely an attempt to discredit her. She had good reason for this belief, as beginning in 1971 Nixon had drawn up an "enemies list" of all his political opponents, and she was on it. This list, which also included every member of the Congressional Black

Caucus, politicians, labor leaders, celebrities, members of the media, business leaders, and academics, became public knowledge during the 1973 Senate Watergate hearings. A year later, the Justice Department cleared her of all charges.

Perhaps, as a result of the investigation, Chisholm began focusing on her own financial security. She was constantly on the road, speaking on college campuses, for women's organizations, and for political clubs, earning more than $30,500 a year in speaker fees. As a consequence, she had the lowest voting attendance record of the entire New York State delegation. Her speaking fees combined with her government salary of $42,500 gave her one of the highest incomes in the House, and she and Conrad were able to build what the *New York Times* described as a "lavish" home in St. Thomas, Virgin Islands.

Along with her concern about her financial security, Chisholm had good reason to worry about the future of the legislative changes of the Great Society. The era of reform politics was clearly at an end, as it was becoming more difficult to pass progressive legislation. The 1970s were marked by economic and social dislocation, as American society was transformed by forces people did not understand and could not control. After twenty-five years of economic growth, wages, employment, and productivity dropped. Recessions were more frequent, and severe inflation soared to a rate of 18 percent. In 1973 an Arab embargo of oil shipments to the United States resulted in a dramatic shortage of gas and oil and marked the end of the post–World War II economic boom. For the first time in forty years, Americans had to wait in hours-long lines to fill up their gas tanks—or do without. This economic dislocation led to the discrediting of the New Deal and Great Society belief in government activism and traditional liberalism and a turn toward the right both politically and socially.

Even though she was on the road and had a poor voting attendance record, she did not turn her back entirely on legislative work. From 1971 to 1977, she served on the Committee on Education and Labor, having won a place on that panel with the help of Democrat Hale Boggs of Louisiana, whom she had endorsed as majority leader over the CBC member John Conyers. She also served on the Committee on Organization Study and Review, whose recommended reforms for the selection of committee chairmen were adopted by the Democratic Caucus in 1971. From 1977 to 1981, Chisholm was secretary of the Democratic Caucus. In 1977 she left her Education Committee assignment to accept a seat on the House Rules Committee, becoming the first black woman—and the second woman ever—to serve on that powerful panel.

But even after six years in Congress, campaigning for the presidency, and serving on national Democratic committees, she still had to insist upon being treated with respect. The committee's presiding officer, James Delaney of Queens, referred to the male committee members as "Mister," but called Chisholm "Shirley." Delaney was shocked when she objected. "Shirley, what's the matter? You and I have been intimate for years," he wondered. Bitingly, she replied, "We don't have to let the public know it." She was Mrs. Chisholm from then on.[1]

After 1972 Chisholm worked closely with a number of feminist congresswomen, including Bella Abzug, Democrat from New York City, and Ella Grasso, from Connecticut. Abzug and Chisholm's relationship was difficult, especially after Chisholm's presidential run. But the two worked together on a common political agenda. After taking the official oath of office for the Ninety-Second Congress, on January 3, 1971, Abzug had taken a "people's oath" on the House steps administered by her New York colleague Shirley Chisholm. Following in Chisholm's footsteps, she also flouted the House rules by refusing her first committee assignment. In 1974 three more women were elected to Congress, including Barbara Jordan, the first African American from the South, and Yvonne Braithwaite (later Braithwaite-Burke), the first African American woman from California. The Ninety-Fourth Congress (1975–1977) had nineteen women representatives, the largest number during Chisholm's tenure. In 1977 she was a founding member of the Congressional Women's Caucus. Along with Braithwaite and Jordan, two African American men were elected, for a total of fifteen African Americans in the House.

After her 1972 reelection, Chisholm's first effort was to save the Office of Economic Opportunity (OEO), the agency responsible for administering most of the War on Poverty programs created as part of President Lyndon B. Johnson's Great Society legislative agenda. VISTA, Job Corps, Community Action Program, and Head Start (later transferred to the Department of Health, Education, and Welfare) were all administered by the OEO. Dating from 1964, it quickly became a target of right-wing critics of the War on Poverty. Nixon was determined to gut the OEO by appointing directors such as Donald Rumsfeld (1969–1971), who was hostile to it, or by impounding appropriated funds. Chisholm agreed with both left- and right-wing critics who charged that there were serious problems with OEO management and that many of its funds had been misappropriated. Yet, as she argued, the overall good its programs did far outweighed these failings.

To mobilize support for the OEO, she forged alliances in Congress, as well as with community groups affected by cuts in the OEO. She called upon the House Education and Labor Committee to conduct hearings in cities across the country. This way, legislators could hear firsthand from the people most affected by its programs. Chisholm conducted these hearings herself and convinced a number of colleagues of the value of the OEO. She had to chuckle at the discomfiture of many of her white colleagues. "Some of them got to the point of confessing that they had never been in a room with so many blacks," she recalled. The hearings served their purpose, for the House voted to continue the OEO. Chisholm "was very proud to have had a role in helping to change attitudes in Congress and helping to save the OEO program."[2] Unfortunately, although Nixon's actions were declared unconstitutional in 1973, successive administrations continued to cut funding.

Chisholm also continued her efforts to have the country's 1.8 million domestic workers covered by minimum-wage laws, often referring to her mother and grandmother, who had worked as domestics. In October 1972, she addressed the founding convention of the National Committee on Household Employment. "We want equal pay for equal work, decent working conditions and respect for the long, hard hours we work," she declared to the "wildly" cheering delegates, overwhelmingly African American women.[3]

Chisholm began this effort by trying to forge a coalition of organized labor, feminists, and African American legislators. She circulated petitions and put supportive remarks about the proposed bill extending the minimum wage to domestic workers into the *Congressional Record*. Creating the coalition was difficult, because there were conflicts between organized labor and NOW. NOW's major legislative priority was passage of the ERA. The American Federation of Labor and Congress of Industrial Organizations historically opposed the ratification of the Equal Rights Amendment, citing concerns that the ERA would eradicate Progressive Era legislation that singled out women workers for special protections. Under pressure from trade-union women, the AFL-CIO reversed its position in 1973. Largely behind the scenes, Chisholm mobilized her aides to work with labor and women's groups. She even went to George Wallace to ask for assistance in winning southern congressional support. Wallace, who never forgot Chisholm's earlier kindness, helped her get the votes of enough southern congressmen to push the legislation through the House.

Her efforts paid off when the House voted 287 to 130 to raise the minimum wage from $1.60 to $2.60 an hour and, for the first time, to extend minimum-wage coverage to domestic workers. Chisholm was very optimistic, not only about the passage of this bill, but also about being able to forge future coalitions and work within the system to pass progressive legislation. But even though the Minimum Wage Bill passed both the House and the Senate, President Nixon vetoed it, claiming it would cause unemployment, increase inflation, and hurt those who could least afford it. Nixon's final (and implausible) rationale was that coverage of domestic household workers was a backward step, for it would result in greater unemployment of domestic workers. Chisholm was furious and discouraged, for it seemed that all her hard work was for nothing.

Together with Bella Abzug, Chisholm introduced another piece of progressive legislation based on her long-term commitment to child care—the most far-reaching day-care bill in the history of Congress. This legislation reflected their ongoing commitment to extending the scope and benefits of the Great Society. Abzug and Chisholm argued that state-subsidized day care would address a real need faced by working mothers, especially since the 1970 census figures showed that fewer than 20 percent of all US households included a male breadwinner and a stay-at-home, non-wage-earning-mother. By providing day-care funds for women at all economic levels, they and other feminists supporting the bill hoped to challenge the prevailing idea that motherhood was the defining role for women. Walter Mondale, Democratic senator from Minnesota, and John Brademas, Democratic representative from Indiana, had also introduced day-care legislation, but Abzug and Chisholm considered that bill inadequate, because it did not cover more than 1,262,400 children under five who were on welfare. Their own bill called for $5 billion in federal subsidies for high-quality day care for families at all levels, to reach $10 billion by 1975; local control over the money so specific community needs could be met; and twenty-four-hour coverage in order to include parents who worked nights. Finally, there were provisions to prohibit sex discrimination in the administration of the bill. The Child Care Bill passed the House and, with Mondale's help, the Senate, only to suffer the same fate as the minimum-wage bill. Nixon vetoed it, claiming it would "Sovietize America's children."

These defeats did more than make Chisholm angry. She began to think of herself as an ineffective legislator and to fear that her hope for a future progressive agenda was doomed. As early as 1973, Chisholm began dropping hints about retiring from politics, if not in 1974, then definitely by 1976. She talked about establishing a political institute that would be affiliated with a number of academic institutions in the Washington, DC, area. "I've visited over 100 campuses, and I've seen that young people want to learn something about politics," she explained.[4] Chisholm also told friends she did not wish to be a career politician, expressing an interest in lecturing, writing, traveling, and spending part of the year at her home in St. Thomas.

The urban centers, largely Democratic Party strongholds, were hit first and hardest by economic turmoil. Even before 1973, cities had faced serious fiscal problems. During the 1960s, millions of middle- and working-class whites had left urban centers. This "white flight" resulted in a declining tax base and a decrease in tax revenues. By 1968, when Chisholm was elected to Congress, cities had a public debt forty times greater than the federal debt. Mayors and state and congressional representatives were faced with having to provide tangible benefits—public schools, housing, safe streets, parks, food stamps, child care—to their constituents even as the amount of funds available for these programs decreased.

This growing economic crisis had racial and gendered political overtones. In 1968 Nixon's campaign had employed a "southern strategy," appealing pointedly to conservative southern white voters still smarting over the victories of the civil rights movement, in particular the Voting Rights Act. He also appealed to white northern workers, many of whom were frightened and alienated by the changes taking place, especially as a result of the black struggle and the feminist movement. Nixon characterized this white constituency as the "silent majority," "the likeminded, the forgotten Americans, the good, decent, taxpaying, law abiding people."[5] Nixon—or, more accurately, his speechwriter William Safire—constantly contrasted these "silent" whites with the noisy minority: African Americans, student and anti–Vietnam War protesters, feminists, and other dissidents.

Other politicians followed his lead, couching the nation's fiscal problems in racialized and gendered code as they attacked the crisis of the urban centers, public schools, a return to "law and order," crime, and welfare. Even after Nixon was forced to resign in disgrace in August 1974, the assault on the cities continued. In that year New York City, the financial capital of the world and the nation's most populous city, stood at the brink of economic collapse. With default virtually a certainty, Gerald Ford, who replaced Nixon, showed Republican disdain for the problems of the big cities and refused to provide any federal funds to help the city. The *New York Daily News* captured the attitude of both the president and an emerging Republican antiurban consensus with the headline "FORD TO CITY: DROP DEAD." But, as it later became apparent, New York's predicament epitomized the problems faced by the nation's other older urban centers.

On top of economic dislocation, the sea changes occurring in women's lives, in family structure, and in sexuality sparked unease and protest. Conservatives began to organize from the grassroots to reestablish patriarchal authority, circumscribe women's sexual freedom, outlaw abortion, and restore "Christian" values. The 1973

Supreme Court *Roe v. Wade* decision legalizing abortion was a catalyst. Conservatives, the Catholic Church, Protestant evangelicals, and others built antiabortion organizations and mobilized their constituents to picket abortion clinics and engage in acts of civil disobedience. Similarly, antihomosexual activists began successful campaigns to oppose antidiscrimination laws. The grassroots conservative movement, often referred to as the "New Right," appealed to millions of Americans who believed in the "traditional values" of the father-centered patriarchal family and wanted American public life to be Christian in character.

The most successful campaign against women's rights, Stop ERA, was led by Phyllis Schlafly, who argued that feminists devalued mothers and the economic security of older married homemakers. Schlafly's organization defeated NOW's attempt to ratify the Equal Rights Amendment and coalesced opposition to every issue of concern to feminists. Women of color and poor women were blamed for poverty, rising crime, drugs, illegitimacy, and single motherhood. Poor women were considered uncaring, inadequate mothers if they worked or lazy welfare cheats if they stayed at home. Working-class and poor women were portrayed as sexually suspect and deserving punishment.

The election of a Democratic president, Jimmy Carter, in 1976 did not make any meaningful difference in the nation's move toward the Right. In the first six months of Carter's presidency, Chisholm met with him to complain that his policies did not do enough to help the urban centers. She pointed out that the federal officials sent to her district were not up to the task of dealing with her constituents. Carter disagreed with Chisholm's position but promised that his next budget would increase services to the poor.

Chisholm disagreed with Carter on a wide range of issues, including reducing the military, public funding for abortion, greater welfare assistance, and more funding for public education, as well as the ill treatment of African American elected officials by Carter's administration. When Ted Kennedy challenged Carter for the primary nomination in 1980, she joined with feminists such as Steinem and Abzug and the Congressional Black Caucus to endorse him. In a significant blow for traditional Democratic Party liberalism, Carter handily defeated Kennedy and then lost the general election to the conservative Ronald Reagan in a landslide.

The 1980 election marked the beginning of a critical rightward shift in the political debate over blacks and women. Reagan began his campaign by expressing support for the ideas of states' rights in Neshoba County, Mississippi, the very place where three civil rights workers had been murdered by the Ku Klux Klan in 1964. His racial message could not have been more obvious. The Republican Party also reversed its previous support for the Equal Rights Amendment, embraced an antiabortion political platform, and demonized poor black women by calling them "welfare queens."

The move to the Right during the 1980s challenged Chisholm's ability to represent her constituency effectively. One political consequence of the fiscal crisis was low voter turnout, especially in the hardest-hit urban areas. In the 1970s and '80s, Chisholm's Bedford-Stuyvesant district, with the highest concentration of African Americans in the country, was also the poorest district and had the lowest voter turnout. The alienation of poor and black voters was not lost on Washington politicians, making it more difficult for Chisholm and other elected officials from poor urban areas to bring federal money into their districts.

A 1980 *New York Times* article headlined "City's Poor Blacks Say That Their Hopes of the 60's Have Dried Up" focused largely on the problems in Bedford-Stuyvesant. It pointed out that the struggles of the 1960s, which forced the national and state governments to prioritize the needs of the urban poor, were now being ignored. Equally distressing, noted the *Times,* was the lack of supportive leadership at the national and mayoral levels, which only increased the district's sense of hopelessness. In the absence of a militant Black Nationalist movement, Brooklyn's black leaders found themselves fighting not over political issues, but rather over who would be the political boss and control what appeared to be a constantly shrinking pie. Carlos Russell, political activist and once dean of contemporary studies at Brooklyn College, explained, "Brooklyn is a mirror of the malady that affects black folks in this country."

The economic crisis and its impact on central Brooklyn was only one factor that added to Chisholm's decision to leave Congress. During her fourteen-year tenure in Washington, Chisholm was a state and local Democratic Party leader, and she used her growing political clout to support and promote friends. For example, at the 1970 New York State Democratic Convention meeting to nominate candidates for governor and lieutenant governor, Chisholm pulled all her political weight to make sure that her friend and ally Basil Paterson got the lieutenant governor slot. She made the argument that Paterson would help the Democratic ticket because of his popularity in New York City. She threatened that if a white person was selected instead of Paterson, there would be reprisals. Arthur Goldberg, who had been US secretary of labor, a Supreme Court justice, and ambassador to the United Nations, was the nominee for governor. The Goldberg-Paterson ticket was defeated by Nelson A. Rockefeller, the incumbent. After the election, some political leaders who had been wary of Paterson's candidacy were forced to admit that Chisholm might have been right and that he had been a bigger asset to the ticket than Goldberg. But having been right about the Paterson candidacy did not endear Chisholm to a number of upstate white Democrats.

The growing rightward shift in US politics, the impact of the economic crisis on the cities, and low voter turnout in Brooklyn meant that Chisholm was not able to provide for her constituents the way she had in the late sixties and early seventies. Political figures who had always disliked and opposed her were beginning to take action to challenge her seat in Congress. She was frustrated by the disaffection of some of her constituents. In 1972 a small number of influential politicians, some of whom had always resented her political prominence and had previously voiced opposition to her presidential campaign, were now raising opposition to her incumbency as a congressperson. The Reverend William A. Jones, for example, pastor of Bethany Baptist Church, one of Brooklyn's largest congregations, and acting national chair of Jesse Jackson's Operation Breadbasket, told the influential *Amsterdam News* that he heard complaints about Chisholm's performance as a representative every day. He intimated that she would probably face a primary run in 1974, which she did. In a very low turnout election, she defeated Clarence Robertson 7,798 to 3,872 and then was overwhelmingly reelected in November. Two years later, she faced a bitter primary fight against Democratic councilman Sam Wright. In this election, Chisholm had the support of some of the better-known black leaders like Percy Sutton, as well as some up-and-coming activists. She won both the primary and the general election handily. But the grumblings continued.

The points of opposition were brought together in a lengthy investigative article in 1978 in the *Village Voice,* coauthored by Andrew Cooper, Chisholm's old political opponent, and journalist Wayne Barrett. Both Cooper and Barrett had been very critical of what they saw as Chisholm's political opportunism from the very beginning of her career. Their *Voice* cover story, headlined "Chisholm's Compromises: Politics and the Art of Self-Interest," presented a critical account of her political behavior. Rather than being the "unbossed," uncompromising fighter for progressive causes, the Brooklyn community, racial justice, and women's rights, Barrett and Cooper charged, Chisholm had done very little for Brooklyn, did not play a positive role in promoting progressive political candidates, and, worse, had not supported black and women candidates. Instead, she had "made a career out of compromise," because she was more interested in self-promotion and political power.[6]

Barrett and Cooper argued that Chisholm's ties to the state Democratic Party machine guided most of her political decisions. For example, they accused her of absenting herself from the 1968 Ocean Hill–Brownsville strike because of her ties to the United Federation of Teachers and the Democratic Party machine. That criticism is unfounded, because during the primary campaign debates with her opponent, James Foreman, Chisholm had unequivocally supported community control of the school district in opposition to the UFT. She had been hospitalized during much of the strike and had also been campaigning for Congress; all these factors certainly explain her absence.

However, Barrett and Cooper's overall analysis of Chisholm's political role is accurate. It complicates the picture Chisholm presented of herself, especially in her autobiography, interviews, and speeches. Chisholm never forgot the lessons she learned as she rose to power in Brooklyn machine politics and was masterful in her ability to combine progressive militant rhetoric with the traditional methods of using the machine to mobilize voters. Chisholm was less interested in attacking the undemocratic nature of the boss system than she was in ensuring the machine's spoils went to her constituents. Especially after her primary campaign for the presidency catapulted her into the national spotlight, she was constantly asked to endorse and campaign for candidates. Time after time, Cooper and Barrett pointed out Chisholm endorsed machine candidates against liberal, progressive, African American, and feminist candidates. Inexplicably, she refused to support the primary campaign of liberal antiwar activist Allard Lowenstein, who in 1972 ran unsuccessfully for Congress in Brooklyn against the local machine candidate, John J. Rooney, a conservative, pro–Vietnam War Democrat who consistently voted against civil rights and social welfare policies. Despite her feminist rhetoric, her record shows that she did not support feminist candidates.

Perhaps her refusal to support Bella Abzug's two primary campaigns—for senator and for mayor—was payback for Abzug's failure to support Chisholm's presidential run. But Chisholm also sat out the 1972 primary race between the strongly anti-ERA House Judiciary Committee chairman, Emanuel Celler—a fifty-year incumbent—and the young feminist attorney Elizabeth Holtzman, who won the election and served for eighteen years. Even more troubling was Chisholm's refusal to support her longtime ally Percy Sutton's failed mayoral campaign in 1977. Instead, she supported the machine candidate and incumbent, Abe Beame, who lost the first primary vote, at which point Chisholm endorsed Congressman Ed Koch in the runoff. Sutton was deeply disappointed. "I believed I could count on her support," he told the *Village Voice*. "I just don't understand Shirley Chisholm." Chisholm angrily defended her support for Koch for mayor in 1977 (and again for governor in 1982) by saying it would give her greater access to federal dollars because she would have "the inside track in New York City and in New York State," if he had won the governorship.[7]

Barrett and Cooper pointed out that Chisholm in fact opposed almost all candidates not backed by Meade Esposito, the long-term Brooklyn Democratic leader and one of the state's most powerful behind-the-scenes politicians until his indictment and conviction for graft in 1977. In that year, she campaigned against Arthur O. Eve, a liberal African American who was running for mayor of Buffalo. Instead, she supported a white conservative Democrat with close ties to Esposito.

Nevertheless, Barrett and Cooper acknowledged that although Chisholm was "bossed," she was not "bought." "She is not a venal woman. She never ripped off a community program, never demanded a cut for herself in patronage or graft. That makes her an unusual politician—black or white." They concluded that Chisholm traded her "independence for a secure base at home," believing that her political security had to be protected by a political machine.

This analysis certainly has a great deal of merit. It is most likely that the Democratic Party machine's support of Chisholm enabled her to stay in Congress by protecting her from primary challenges. In return for her loyalty to the machine, she could continue to be outspoken and provocative. Barrett and Cooper do not fully take into account the precariousness of Chisholm's political position, due in part to her class, race, gender, and status of being a "first." Chisholm had to battle politically in a white man's political world, where daggers were out at all times and political alliances were constantly changing. It is true that she made a number of political decisions that contradicted her professed support of liberal and progressive people and causes. But she may have felt she had no choice if she wanted to pursue her long-term progressive goals. She never really responded to the *Voice* attack except to remind everyone that Cooper and Barrett had been her longtime political adversaries, that men had always been angered by her success, and that her idea of being "unbossed" meant that she had every right to choose alliances and endorsements—something she had always done since her first days as an Albany legislator.

Along with the changes in her political life, her personal life was undergoing a dramatic transformation. Sometime during the 1970s, her marriage began to falter. Conrad Chisholm's devotion to her made him a beloved figure in Brooklyn and Washington. He would pick her up at the airport, take her back home to Brooklyn, cook delicious Jamaican dishes, and make sure that his wife had time to rest. Everyone who knew them described them as a happily devoted, fun-loving couple. But over time, Shirley's fame began to get to Conrad. He was never Conrad Chisholm, successful private investigator, but Conrad Chisholm, Shirley Chisholm's "wife." He began to visit Washington less frequently, preferring to be with his friends and neighbors in Brooklyn. Shirley Chisholm attributed their breakup to the stresses of politics. She and Conrad had an amicable divorce. He moved to the Virgin Islands but always stayed close to Chisholm and her sisters, and Chisholm remembered him in her will

At age fifty-three, Shirley Chisholm was also restless and even while still married began dating. According to a number of her friends and staffers, she prided herself on her slim figure, her flirtatious demeanor, and her ability to attract men. She became involved with Arthur Hardwick Jr., a Buffalo businessman who had been in the New York State Assembly with Chisholm and had lost his seat in 1966 to Arthur O. Eve (perhaps that helps explain Chisholm's opposition to Eve in the mayoral primary in 1977). She married Hardwick on Thanksgiving Day 1977, and from then on divided her time between Washington, her Brooklyn district, and Buffalo. Her marriage to Hardwick increased the grumbling in Brooklyn. Calling her the Brooklyn congresswoman from Buffalo, her detractors claimed she was spending too much time away from Brooklyn and Washington, a charge she vehemently denied, pointing out that in her first four years of marriage to Hardwick, she had spent a total of only forty-two days in Buffalo.

In 1982 Chisholm announced that she would not seek reelection. Wayne Barrett and other columnists believed she was stepping down because she feared she would face a primary challenge and probably lose. No doubt that was a major factor in her decision. Given Chisholm's intense belief in herself, she most likely felt it would be too much of a defeat for the iconic first African American woman elected to Congress, and first African American and first woman to mount a campaign for president, to lose a congressional primary. However,

Chisholm cited other factors, primarily the current political climate. Defiant and defensive, she asserted that the Reagan presidency and the quiescence of Democratic politicians made it next to impossible to fight for the services needed by her largely black and impoverished constituency. Chisholm claimed she had wanted to leave earlier, but felt obligated to stay on, especially after the departure of her two African American congressional sisters, Yvonne Braithwaite-Burke and Barbara Jordan.

She gave personal reasons for leaving as well. In 1978 her husband was in a horrific automobile accident, and during the ten months of his hospitalization, Chisholm had to be in Washington. "Fortunately he has recovered. Now I want to spend more time with my family."[8] As expected, the announcement of her retirement was national news. But Chisholm promised she would not disappear. "My voice will still be heard, but not as an elected official," she said, and assured everyone that "that this is not a funeral, politically."[9]

11

Conclusion

"I am at peace with myself. It's been a remarkable challenge. I am not looking back," Chisholm reflected as she prepared to leave office. In numerous interviews after giving up her seat, she said she had received thousands of letters from her constituents as well as people all over the country asking, "Why are you deserting us? Why are you leaving us?"

She may have thought she was at peace, but these interviews reveal someone who was quite angry about the overall political situation and her own difficulties as a legislator. In interview after interview, she reiterated that the Reagan administration made it impossible for her to be responsive to her constituency. "I am not going to lie," she said. "Many of us can't be effective at this time. It's not because we're not trying but because the gods seem to be against us." She also lashed out at the double—actually triple—standard applied to her as a woman and as an African American politician. Responding to the charge that she lived part-time in Buffalo, she asked whether "white people care about where their representatives live," pointing out that James Buckley lived in Connecticut when he was a senator from New York and that New York senator Robert Kennedy lived in Massachusetts.

She was also furious over the charges of absenteeism, especially after her husband was injured in an accident in Buffalo. Claiming that she was damned for abdicating her gendered role as a devoted wife and staying in Washington, she explained that she was the only woman and the only African American sitting on the House Rules Committee as important legislation concerning women and racial minorities moved toward a vote. Had she left to be with her husband, she would have been accused of deserting her political responsibilities. Repeating her oft-quoted comment that being a woman was a bigger handicap than being black, she described how people said to her, "If you were a black male, with your accomplishments, your versatility, your charisma, your everything—boy, you'd be riding high in this country today. You'd be an acknowledged black leader. But, as a woman, you'll never make it."

After her retirement from Congress, she was feted by the Congressional Black Caucus, her constituents in Brooklyn, and her friends in Washington. But she left Washington and Brooklyn a figure of continuing controversy. Major Owens, former president of Brooklyn CORE and state assemblyman, who was elected in 1982 to fill Chisholm's seat, accused her of "acting like a conspirator with the white power structure. She'll make a pact with anyone." Julius Lester, noted civil rights activist, author, professional comedian, and professor of Afro-American studies at the University of Massachusetts, had a more measured view: he pointed out that she used her "position and visibility to be a spokeswoman in a way that no one else in the Congressional Black Caucus has done." What these critics did not understand, Chisholm responded, "is that I've lasted for 25 years out there in the political arena—because someone out there likes what I've been doing. . . . I've delivered in spite of the controversy—because I know how to play the game."[1] Again, this statement reflects the contradictions that Chisholm faced, a progressive Democrat who in a very difficult political period had to make deals and compromises with more conservative politicians in order to serve her constituents as well as possible.

Her political enemies in New York were able to thwart many of her hopes for life after Congress. Seeing herself primarily as an educator, she had always hoped to be offered a college presidency, especially since Medgar Evers College of the City University of New York, to be located in her former district, Crown Heights, Brooklyn, was then in the planning stages. Various community organizations, including the

Bedford-Stuyvesant Restoration Corporation, the Central Brooklyn Coordinating Council, and the NAACP, and local elected officials in Central Brooklyn played a central role in designing the college. However, she had made opponents during her political career who opposed the notion of her being the first president of Medgar Evers College. Although Chisholm was disappointed that she was not a candidate for president, she continued to support the institution.

In 1978 Chisholm was approached by Mayor Koch to consider being the chancellor of the New York City Public Schools. Even before she formally submitted her application, Albert Shanker, the very powerful president of both the New York United Federation of Teachers and its parent body, the American Federation of Teachers, and her longtime political foe, dating back to the Ocean Hill–Brownsville struggle, threatened to veto Koch's school bills if she was appointed. Knowing that she would face significant Republican opposition as well, she withdrew her candidacy. In 1981 she was one of three finalists for the presidency of City College of New York, but again, because of influential political opposition, was passed over.

However, she was also offered a number of academic, corporate, and journalist positions. Now fifty-eight, Chisholm chose to teach and, having turned down positions at Howard, Spelman, and ten other colleges, accepted an offer to become the Purington Professor of Politics at Mount Holyoke College, an all-women's college in South Hadley, Massachusetts. She was following in the footsteps of other prestigious Purington Professors, including Bertrand Russell, W. H. Auden, and Arna Bontemps. Chisholm had spoken at Mount Holyoke in 1971 and had been its commencement speaker in 1981, when she received an honorary degree. At that commencement, she shared the dais with Rosa Parks, who was also honored. The Mount Holyoke dean of faculty immediately suggested to then president Elizabeth Kennan Burns that they invite Chisholm to teach there. At a series of initial meetings with the congresswoman on campus, the dean recalled, a group of students asked her for advice on becoming social activists. "Learn how to raise money," she told them.

Chisholm came to Mount Holyoke in 1983 to teach politics and sociology. She was cognizant of Mount Holyoke's historical importance: "Maybe subconsciously I was attracted here because I was the first black woman to be elected to the United State House of Representatives and this is the oldest all-female college in the country." When a reporter asked why she—daughter of immigrants, working-class woman from Brooklyn, former schoolteacher and child-care worker—would want to resume her teaching career at a private all-female college with predominantly upper-class white students, she explained that she relished that particular challenge. She pointed out that as an African American woman who was part of the feminist movement and a successful member of Congress, she hoped to "open up the eyes and enhance the understanding of these young women here who have come from very protected sheltered atmospheres, and have not had experiences in the real wide pragmatic naked world."[2]

Cecelia Hartsel, now an entrepreneur and graduate student at Fordham University in New York, took classes from Chisholm at Mount Holyoke. Her mother urged her to take the classes and even threatened her daughter that she would drive up from Tennessee to South Hadley to audit Professor Chisholm's classes. Hartsel remembers being in awe of her, but that she "was very kind and put everyone at ease, while peppering lectures with stories from her campaigns and other life experiences. Her stories were amazing, because they literally brought the prior fifty years to life for us—the good, the bad and the ugly." Hartsel concluded that Chisholm was "one of my most influential professors, at a college which gave me lifelong friendships forged over M&C's [macaroni and cheese], as well as a capacity to think more broadly, and the desire to leave the world a better place than I found it."[3]

Living in South Hadley three days a week, and then in Buffalo with her ailing husband, was very trying. But the days in South Hadley, especially after her grueling Washington schedule, became her refuge. "Here in these quiet towns, there is nothing to do, so I read a lot," she told a reporter. "For years I have been reading because of politics. I never read for pleasure. Now I'm reading some fascinating books, autobiographies and biographies and novels, things that I want to do."[4] She taught classes in American political systems and the social roles of women and found herself surrounded by admiring students and faculty. She was interviewed by all the local newspapers and invited to speak at the neighboring colleges. She attended conferences and seminars at Mount Holyoke with leading actors in the black freedom struggle, such as Dr. Betty Shabazz, Malcolm X's widow, and South African activist Dennis Brutus. She attended a Mount Holyoke–sponsored seminar in Senegal. On occasion, she managed to stir up controversy. In 1983, while giving a speech called "Women in Motion" to two hundred students at Our Lady of Elms College in the neighboring town of Chicopee, she was greeted by two hundred antiabortion protesters.

She did not give up her passion for politics even while teaching. In 1984 she helped found the National Political Congress of Black Women and campaigned for Jesse Jackson's presidential nomination in 1984 and 1988. In 1987 her friend and mentee Donna Brazile, the political commentator and Democratic Party activist, encouraged her to join with activists such as Loretta Ross and spoke at the first national conference of Women of Color and Reproductive Rights in 1987.

After her husband died in 1986, Chisholm taught one year at Spelman College in Atlanta and then in 1991 moved to Palm Coast, Florida, where she lectured and wrote occasional op-ed pieces. In 1993 President Clinton offered Chisholm the post of ambassador to Jamaica, but she declined due to ill health. She died on New Year's Day 2005.

At the time of her death, her reputation as a political trailblazer, fierce champion of her Bedford-Stuyvesant community, and fighter against racism and for women's rights had faded. In fact, she was all but erased from historical memory. The mainstream media, the constituents of her former congressional district, college students, post-1960s feminists, and political activists—none knew her history. Shirley Chisholm was not taught in the schools. Even feminists under the age of fifty hardly knew who she was, and as of this writing the only biographies of her are children's books. When the Brooklyn College Women's Studies faculty met in 2004 to consider naming a research center after her, most did not know she was an alumna, and a few did not even know who she was. Brooklyn College students, some of whom benefited from the SEEK program that Chisholm initiated, had never heard of her.

A central reason for Chisholm's erasure from public memory is part of the nation's legacy of race and gender discrimination. It is clear that the lives of working-class women of color are less valued than those of influential white men. Even nationally known African American women's lifelong activism gets distorted: Rosa Parks was portrayed as just a tired seamstress, Coretta Scott King as only a grieving widow. There were other reasons as well for Chisholm's disappearance. When she died, she had not lived in Brooklyn for more than twenty years and before then had alienated, opposed, or offended many of the Brooklyn politicians who were now in positions of power and had little reason to sing her praises.

The mainstream media also helped keep Chisholm's story out of public awareness. During the hotly contested 2008 Democratic presidential primary between an African American man, Barack Obama, and a white woman, Hillary Clinton, when issues of gender and race were fiercely and bitterly debated, there was no mention of Chisholm. Very few pundits referred to her campaign as opening the door for Hillary Clinton or the eventual historic election of President Barack Obama.

Yet at the same time, politicians, filmmakers, and a new generation of social justice scholar-activists were beginning to seriously reconsider Chisholm's legacy. In 2005 Shola Lynch's documentary *Chisholm 72: Unbought and Unbossed* brought Chisholm back to a national audience. The film, an account of her presidential run, was widely screened, won a prestigious Peabody Award, and was shown at the 2008 Democratic National Convention. Today, a growing number of scholars are developing an interest in critically reassessing Chisholm, along with women of color in the black struggle, the civil rights movement in the North, Lyndon Johnson's Great Society, and the social history of Brooklyn. Her life and legacy are frequent topics at academic conferences across the country.

Meanwhile, national and local politicians—including some who never worked with Chisholm—have begun to honor her. Immediately after her death, Brooklyn state assemblyman Nick Perry introduced legislation making November 30, Chisholm's birthday, Shirley Chisholm Day in New York State. She is the first woman to have a state holiday named after her. In 2009 the Speaker of the House, Democrat Nancy Pelosi (the first woman to hold that position), joined Barbara Lee, chair of the Congressional Black Caucus and former Chisholm for President campaign worker, and Yvette Clarke, who holds Chisholm's old congressional seat, to unveil Kadir Nelson's portrait of Chisholm in the Capitol. "With this portrait, we make certain that when the story is told about some of the most critical struggles in our nation's history—the unending fight for the ideal of equality that is both our nation's heritage and our hope—Shirley Chisholm's name is remembered," Pelosi said.[5] Public intellectuals and political commentators such as CNN's Donna Brazile and MSNBC's Melissa Harris-Perry invoke Chisholm's words and actions in their blogs and on the airwaves.

Like her life, Chisholm's legacy remains complicated and contentious, because her political agenda calling for a larger social welfare system, national health care, expanded access to public education, feminism, and opposition to racism and wars continues to be fought over on the national stage. At the same time, her political history emphasizes the enormous obstacles that outspoken political reformers face when trying to work within the American political system. Does one work in Congress as an advocate for social causes or as a career legislator who often compromises with political opponents? As one who worked within the Democratic Party, Chisholm often referred to Malcolm X's famous phrase "the ballot or the bullet," and clearly she saw her political choice as the ballot.

Chisholm was outspoken in her support for both women and racial minorities. She was forthright in challenging the sexism among African Americans and the racism within the feminist movement. Her feminism was connected to all contemporary social issues: ending the war in Vietnam, abolishing poverty, opposing racialized police and state violence, and expansion of social welfare programs, including education, day care, and health care. She constantly reminded her audiences that these issues connect race and gender, and she defined them as feminist issues of concern to all women, but especially to women of color because "they are subject to more discrimination than whites." Her commitment to feminism never wavered, and she thanked and credited the women's movement for so much of the social progress that occurred during her eighteen years as an elected official.

Yet her most famous quote, "Of my two handicaps, being female puts more obstacles in my path than being black," continues to be hotly debated, in part because the historic schism between white feminists and black activists has not been resolved. During the heated 2008 Democratic primary between two potential "firsts," the media and Obama and Clinton supporters both took this phrase out of its historical context. Obama supporters claimed that Obama was victimized because of race, while Clinton loyalists claimed that gender was the most restrictive force in American politics. One side privileged race over gender, the other gender over race, in a struggle to claim its candidate was the most victimized. By pitting one against the other, they missed the opportunity to examine how race and gender intersect. A true espousal of Shirley Chisholm's lifelong legacy would be building a multiracial, intergenerational, inclusive coalition as a powerful force for social change.

Amid all these complimentary and contradictory views of her, here is how Chisholm summed up her legacy. In an interview in 2004, she said that she wanted "history to remember me not just as the first black woman to be elected to Congress, not as the first black woman to have made a bid for the presidency of the United States, but as a black woman who lived in the 20th century and dared to be herself. I want to be remembered as a catalyst for change."

PRIMARY DOCUMENTS

FACING THE ABORTION QUESTION

FROM *UNBOUGHT AND UNBOSSED* BY SHIRLEY CHISHOLM

In August of 1969 I started to get phone calls from NARAL, the National Association for the Repeal of Abortion Laws, a new organization based in New York City that was looking for a national president. In the New York State Assembly I had supported abortion reform bills introduced by Assemblyman Albert Blumenthal, and this had apparently led NARAL to believe I would sympathize with its goal: complete repeal of all laws restricting abortion. As a matter of fact, when I was in the Assembly I had not been in favor of repealing all abortion laws, a step that would leave the question of having or not having the operation entirely up to a woman and her doctor. The bills I had tried to help pass in Albany would only have made it somewhat easier for women to get therapeutic abortions in New York State, by providing additional legal grounds and simplifying the procedure for getting approval. But since that time I had been compelled to do some heavy thinking on the subject, mainly because of the experiences of several young women I knew. All had suffered permanent injuries at the hands of illegal abortionists. Some will never have children as a result. One will have to go to a hospital periodically for treatment for the rest of her life.

It had begun to seem to me that the question was not whether the law should allow abortion. Experience shows that pregnant women who feel they have compelling reasons for not having a baby, or another baby, will break the law and, even worse, risk injury and death if they must to get one.

Abortions will not be stopped. It may even be that the number performed is not being greatly reduced by laws making an abortion a "criminal operation." If that is true, the question becomes simply that of what kind of abortions society wants women to have— clean, competent ones performed by licensed physicians or septic, dangerous ones done by incompetent practitioners.

So when NARAL asked me to lead its campaign, I gave it serious thought. For me to take the lead in abortion repeal would be an even more serious step than for a white politician to do so, because there is a deep and angry suspicion among many blacks that even birth control clinics are a plot by the white power structure to keep down the numbers of blacks, and this opinion is even more strongly held by some in regard to legalizing abortions. But I do not know any black or Puerto Rican women who feel that way. To label family planning and legal abortion programs "genocide" is male rhetoric, for male ears. It falls flat to female listeners, and to thoughtful ones too. Women know, and so do many men, that two or three children who are wanted, prepared for, reared amid love and stability, and educated to the limit of their ability will mean more for the future of the black and brown races from which they come than any number of neglected, hungry, ill-housed and ill-clothed youngsters. Pride in one's race, as well as simple humanity, supports this view. Poor women of every race feel as I do, I believe. There is objective evidence of it in a study by Dr. Charles F. Westhoff of the Princeton Office of Population Research. He questioned 5,600 married persons and found that 22 percent of their children were unwanted. But among persons who earn less than $4,000 a year, 42 percent of the children were unwanted. The poor are more anxious about family planning than any other group.

Why then do the poor keep on having large families? It is not because they are stupid or immoral. One must understand how many resources their poverty has deprived them of, and that chief among these is medical care and advice. The poor do not go to doctors or clinics except when they absolutely must; their medical ignorance is very great, even when compared to the low level of medical knowledge most persons have. This includes, naturally, information about contraceptives and how to get them. In some of the largest cities, clinics are now attacking this problem; they are nowhere near to solving it. In smaller cities and in most of the countryside, hardly anything is being done.

Another point is this: not only do the poor have large families, but also large families tend to be poor. More than one fourth of all the families with four children live in poverty, according to the federal government's excessively narrow definition; by humane standards of poverty, the number would be much larger. The figures range from 9 percent of one-child families that have incomes below the official poverty line, up to 42 percent of the families with six children or more. Sinking into poverty, large families tend to stay there because of the educational and social handicaps that being poor imposes. It is the fear of such a future for their children that drives many women, of every color and social stratum, except perhaps the highest, to seek abortions when contraception has failed.

Botched abortions are the largest single cause of death of pregnant women in the United States, particularly among nonwhite women. In 1964, the president of the New York County Medical Society, Dr. Carl Goldmark, estimated that 80 percent of the deaths of gravid women in Manhattan were from this cause.

Another study by Edwin M. Gold, covering 1960 through 1962, gave lower percentages but supplied evidence that women from minority groups suffer most. Gold said abortion was the cause of death in 25 percent of the white cases, 49 percent of the black ones, and 65 percent of the Puerto Rican ones.

Even when a poor woman needs an abortion for the most impeccable medical reasons, acceptable under most states' laws, she is not likely to succeed in getting one. The public hospitals to which she must go are far more reluctant to approve abortions than are private, voluntary hospitals. It's in the records: private hospitals in New York City perform 3.9 abortions for every 1000 babies they deliver, public hospitals only 1 per 1000. Another relevant figure is that 90 percent of the therapeutic abortions in the city are performed on white women. Such statistics convinced me that my instinctive feeling was right: a black woman legislator, far from avoiding the abortion question, was compelled to face it and deal with it.

But my time did not permit me to be an active president of NARAL, so I asked to be made an honorary president. My appearances on television in September 1969, when the association's formation was announced, touched off one of the heaviest flows of mail to my Washington office that I have experienced. What surprised me was that it was overwhelmingly in favor of repeal. Most of the letters that disagreed with me were from Catholics, and most of them were temperate and reasoned. We sent those writers a reply that said in part, "No one should be forced to have an abortion or to use birth control methods which for religious or personal reasons they oppose. But neither should others who have different views be forced to abide by what they do not and cannot believe in." Some of the mail was from desperate women who thought I could help them. "I am forty-five years old," one wrote, "and have raised a family already. Now I find that I am pregnant and I need help. Please send me all the information." A girl wrote that she was pregnant and did not dare tell her mother and stepfather: "Please send me the name of a doctor or hospital that would help. You said if my doctor wouldn't do it to write to you. Where can I turn?" We sent the writers of these letters a list of the names and addresses of the chapters of the Clergy Consultation Service on Abortion and suggested that they find a local family planning or birth control clinic.

The reaction of a number of my fellow members of Congress seemed to me a little strange. Several said to me, "This abortion business . . . my God, what are you doing? That's not politically wise." It was the same old story; they were not thinking in terms of right or wrong, they were considering only whether taking a side of the issue would help them stay in office—or in this case, whether taking a stand would help me get reelected. They concluded that it would not help me, so it was a bad position for me to take. My advisers were, of course, all men. So I decided to shake them up a little with a feminist line of counterattack. "Who told you I shouldn't do this?" I asked them. "Women are dying every day, did you know that? They're being butchered and maimed. No matter what men think, abortion is a fact of life. Women will have them; they always have and always will. Are they going to have good ones or bad ones? Will the good ones be reserved for the rich while poor women have to go to quacks? Why don't we talk about real problems instead of phony ones?"

One member asked the question that was on the minds of all the others: "How many Catholics do you have in your district?" "Look," I told him, "I can't worry about that. That's not the problem." Persons who do not deal with politicians are often baffled by the peculiarly simple workings of their minds. Scientists and scholars in particular are bewildered by the political approach. When a member of Congress makes a statement, the scholar's first thought is "Is what he said true? Is he right or wrong?" The falseness or validity of an officeholder's statement is almost never discussed in Washington, or anyplace where politics sets the tone of discourse. The question political people ask is seldom "Is he right?" but "Why did he say that?" Or they ask, "Where does he expect that to get him?" or "Who put him up to that?"

But returning to abortion, the problem that faced me was what action I should take in my role as a legislator, if any; naturally, I intended to be as active as possible as an advocate and publicist for the cause, but was there any chance of getting a meaningful bill through Congress? Some NARAL officials wanted me to introduce an abortion repeal bill as a gesture. This is very common; probably a majority of the bills introduced in all legislative bodies are put in for the sake of effect, to give their sponsor something to talk about on the stump. That was never my style in Albany, and I have not adopted it in Washington. When I introduce legislation, I try to draft it carefully and then look for meaningful support from people who have the power to help move the bill.

So I looked for House members, in both parties and of all shades of conservatism and liberalism, who might get together on abortion repeal regardless of party. I wrote letters to a number of the more influential House members. It would have been easy to get three or four, or even ten or twelve, liberal Democrats to join me in introducing a bill, but nothing would have happened. A majority of House members would have said, "Oh, that bunch again," and dismissed us. But just a few conservative Republican co-sponsors, or conservative Democratic ones, would change all that. The approach I took was eminently sound, but it didn't work. A few members replied that they would support my bill if it ever got to the floor, but could not come out for it publicly before then or work for it. I did not doubt their sincerity, but it was a safe thing to say because the chances of a bill's reaching the floor seemed slim. Several others answered with longish letters admiring my bold position and expressing sympathy, but not agreement. "I am not ready to assume such a position," one letter said. Another said, in almost these words, "This kind of trouble I don't need." So I put my roughly drafted bill in a drawer and decided to wait. There is no point in introducing it until congressmen can be persuaded to vote for it, and only one thing will persuade them. If a congressman feels he is in danger of losing his job, he will change his mind—and then try to make it look as though he had been leading the way. The approach to Congress has to be through the arousal and organization of public opinion.

The question will remain "Is abortion *right?*" and it is a question that each of us must answer for himself. My beliefs and my experience have led me to conclude that the wisest public policy is to place the responsibility for that decision on the individual. The rightness or wrongness of an abortion depends on the individual case, and it seems to me clearly wrong to pass laws regulating all cases. But there is more to it than that. First, it is my view, and I think the majority's view, that abortion should always remain a last resort, never a primary method of limiting families. Contraceptive devices are the first choice: *devices*, because of their established safety compared to the controversial oral contraceptives. The weight of responsible medical opinion, by which I mean the opinions of qualified persons who have never been in the pay of the drug industry, seems to be that the question of the Pill's safety is not proven and that there are clear warnings that much more study is needed. So Pill research should continue, and meanwhile the emphasis—particularly in a publicly supported family planning program—should be on proven safe and effective methods. Beyond that, still from the standpoint of public policy, there must be far more stress on providing a full range of family planning services to persons of all economic levels. At present, the full gamut of services, from expert medical advice to, as a last resort, safe "legal" abortions, is available for the rich. Any woman who has the money and the sophistication about how things are done in our society can get an abortion within the law. If she is from a social stratum where such advice is available, she will be sent to a sympathetic psychiatrist and he will be well paid to believe her when she says she is ready to kill herself if she doesn't get rid of her pregnancy. But unless a woman has the $700 to $1,000 minimum it takes to travel this route, her only safe course in most states is to have the child.

This means that, whether it was so intended, public policy as expressed in American abortion laws (excepting the handful of states where the repeal effort has succeeded) is to maximize illegitimacy. Illegitimate children have always been born and for the foreseeable future they will continue to be. Their handicap is not some legal blot on their ancestry; few intelligent persons give any thought to that today. The trouble is that illegitimate children are usually the most unwanted of the unwanted. Society has forced a woman to have a child in order to punish her. Our laws were based on the Puritan reaction of "You've had your pleasure—now pay for it." But who pays? First it is the helpless woman, who may be a girl in her early teens forced to assume the responsibility of an adult; young, confused, partially educated, she is likely to be condemned to society's trash heap as a result. But the child is often a worse loser. If his mother keeps him, she may marry or not (unmarried mothers are even less likely to marry than widows or divorcées). If she does not, she will have to neglect him and work at undesirable jobs to feed him, more often than not. His homelife will almost certainly be abnormal; he may survive it and even thrive, depending on his mother's personal qualities, but the odds have to be against him.

Of course, there should be no unwanted children. Whether they are legitimate or illegitimate is not of the first importance. But we will not even approach the ideal of having every child wanted, planned for, and cherished, until our methods of contraception are fully reliable and completely safe, and readily available to everyone. Until then, unwanted pregnancies will happen, in marriage and out of it. What is our public policy to be toward them? There are very few more important questions for society to face; this question is one that government has always avoided because it did not dare intrude on the sanctity of the home and marriage. But the catastrophic perils that follow in the train of overpopulation were not well known in the past and those perils were not imminent, so the question could be ducked. It cannot be any longer.

For all Americans, and especially for the poor, we must put an end to compulsory pregnancy. The well-off have only one problem when an unwanted pregnancy occurs; they must decide what they want to do and what they believe is right. For the poor, there is no such freedom. They started with too little knowledge about contraception, often with none except street lore and other misinformation. When trapped by pregnancy, they have only two choices, both bad—a cheap abortion or an unwanted child to plunge them deeper into poverty. Remember the statistics that show which choice is often taken: 49 percent of the deaths of pregnant black women and 65 percent of those of Puerto Rican women . . . due to criminal, amateur abortions.

Which is more like genocide, I have asked some of my black brothers—this, the way things are, or the conditions I am fighting for in which the full range of family planning services is freely available to women of all classes and colors, starting with effective contraception and extending to safe, legal termination of undesired pregnancies, at a price they can afford?

WOMEN AND THEIR LIBERATION

FROM *UNBOUGHT AND UNBOSSED* BY SHIRLEY CHISHOLM

When a young woman graduates from college and starts looking for a job, one question every interviewer is sure to ask her is "Can you type?" There is an entire system of prejudice unspoken behind that question, which is rarely if ever asked of a male applicant. One of my top assistants in my Washington office has always refused to learn to type, although not knowing how has been an inconvenience, because she refused to let herself be forced into a dead-end clerical job.

Why are women herded into jobs as secretaries, librarians, and teachers and discouraged from being managers, lawyers, doctors, and members of Congress? Because it is assumed that they are different from men. Today's new militant campaigners for women's rights have made the point that for a long time society discriminated against blacks on the same basis: they were different and inferior. The cheerful old darky on the plantation and the happy little homemaker are equally stereotypes drawn by prejudice. White America is beginning to be able to admit that it carries racial prejudice in its heart, and that understanding marks the beginning of the end of racism. But prejudice against women is still acceptable because it is invisible. Few men can be persuaded to believe that it exists. Many women, even, are the same way. There is very little understanding yet of the immorality involved in double pay scale and the classification of the better jobs "for men only." More than half the population of the United States is female, but women occupy only 2 percent of the managerial positions. They have not yet even reached the level of tokenism. No woman has ever sat on the Supreme Court, or the AFL-CIO council. There have been only two women who have held cabinet rank, and at present there are none. Only two women now hold ambassadorial rank in the diplomatic corps. In Congress, there are one woman senator and ten representatives. Considering that there are about 3.5 million more women in the United States than men, this is outrageous.

It is true that women have seldom been aggressive in demanding their rights and so have cooperated in their own enslavement. This was true of the black population for many years. They submitted to oppression, and even condoned it. But women are becoming aware, as blacks did, that they can have equal treatment if they will fight for it, and they are starting to organize. To do it, they have to dare the sanctions that society imposes on anyone who breaks with its traditions. This is hard, and especially hard for women, who are taught not to rebel from infancy, from the time they are first wrapped in pink blankets, the color of their caste. Another disability is that women have been programmed to be dependent on men. They seldom have economic freedom enough to let them be free in more significant ways, at least until they become widows and most of their lives are behind them.

That there are no female Supreme Court justices is important, but not as important as the fact that ordinary working women by the millions are subjected to the most naked and unjustified discrimination, by being confined to the duller and less well-paid jobs or by being paid less than men for doing the same work. Here are a recent year's figures from the Labor Department: white males earned an average of $7,179 a year, black males $4,508, white women $4,142, and black women $2,934. Measured in uncontestable dollars and cents, which is worse—race prejudice or antifeminism? White women are at an economic disadvantage even compared to black men, and black women are nowhere on the earnings scale.

Guidance counselors discriminate against girls just as they have long done with young black or Puerto Rican male students. They advise a black boy to prepare for a service oriented occupation, not a profession. They steer a girl toward her "natural career," of being a wife and mother, and plan an occupational goal for her that will not interfere too much with that aim. The girl responds just as the average young black does, with mute agreement. Even if she feels vaguely rebellious at the limitations being put on her future before it has even begun, she knows how the cards are stacked against her and she gives in.

Young minority-group people do not get this treatment quite as much as they did, because they have been radicalized and the country has become more sensitive to its racist attitudes and the damage they do. Women too must rebel. They should start in school, by rejecting the traditional education society considers suitable to them, and which amounts to educational, social, and economic slavery.

There are relevant laws on the books, just as there are civil rights laws on the books. In the 91st Congress, I am a sponsor of the perennial Equal Rights Amendment, which has been before every Congress for the last forty years but has never passed the House. It would outlaw any discrimination on the basis of sex. Men and women would be completely equal before the law. But laws will not solve deep-seated problems overnight. Their use is to provide shelter for those who are most abused, and to begin an evolutionary process by compelling the insensitive majority to reexamine its unconscious attitudes.

The law cannot do the major part of the job of winning equality for women. Women must do it themselves. They must become revolutionaries. Against them is arrayed the weight of centuries of tradition, from St. Paul's "Let women learn in silence" down to the American adage, "A woman's place is in the home." Women have been persuaded of their own inferiority; too many of them believe the male fiction that they are emotional, illogical, unstable, inept with mechanical things, and lack leadership ability.

The best defense against this slander is the same one blacks have found. While they were ashamed of their color, it was an albatross hanging around their necks. They freed themselves from that dead weight by picking up their blackness and holding it out proudly for all the world to see. They found their own beauty and turned their former shame into their badge of honor. Women should perceive that the negative attitudes they hold toward their own femaleness are the creation of an antifeminist society, just as the black shame at being black was the product of racism. Women should start to replace their negative ideas of their femininity with positive ones affirming their nature more and more strongly.

It is not female egotism to say that the future of mankind may very well be ours to determine. It is a fact. The warmth, gentleness, and compassion that are part of the female stereotype are positive human values, values that are becoming more and more important as the values of our world begin to shatter and fall from our grasp. The strength of Christ, Gandhi, and Martin Luther King was a strength of gentleness, understanding, and compassion, with no element of violence in it. It was, in short, a female strength, and that is the kind that often marks the highest type of man.

If we reject our restricted roles, we do not have to reject these values of femaleness. They are enduring values, and we must develop the capacity to hold them and to dispense them to those around us. We must become revolutionaries in the style of Gandhi and King. Then, working toward our own freedom, we can help the others work free from the traps of their stereotypes. In the end, antiblack, antifemale, and all forms of discrimination are equivalent to the same thing—antihumanism. The values of life must be maintained against the enemies in every guise. We can do it by confronting people with their own humanity and their own inhumanity whenever we meet them, in the streets, in school, in church, in bars, in the halls of legislatures. We must reject not only the stereotypes that others have of us but also those that we have of ourselves and others.

In particular, I am certain that more and more American women must become involved in politics. It could be the salvation of our nation. If there were more women in politics, it would be possible to start cleaning it up. Women I have known in government have seemed to me to be much more apt to act for the sake of a principle or moral purpose. They are not as likely as men to engage in deals, manipulations, and sharp tactics. A larger proportion of women in Congress and every other legislative body would serve as a reminder that the real purpose of politicians is to work for the people.

The woman who gets into politics will find that the men who are already there will treat her as the high school counselor treats girls. They see her as someone who is obviously just playing at politics part-time, because after all, her real place is at home being a wife and mother. I suggested a bright young woman as a candidate in New York City a while ago; she had unlimited potential and with good management and some breaks could become an important person to the city. A political leader rejected her: "Why invest all the time and effort to build up the gal into a household name," he asked me, "when she's pretty sure to drop out of the game to have a couple of kids at just about the time we're ready to run her for mayor?"

Many women have given their lives to political organizations, laboring anonymously in the background while men of far less ability managed and mismanaged the public trust. These women hung back because they knew the men would not give them a chance. They knew their place and stayed in it. The amount of talent that has been lost to our country that way is appalling. I think one of my major uses is as an example to the women of our country, to show them that if a woman has ability, stamina, organizational skill, and a knowledge of the issues she can win public office. And if I can do it, how much more hope should that give to white women, who have only one handicap?

One distressing thing is the way men react to women who assert their equality: their ultimate weapon is to call them unfeminine. They think she is anti-male; they even whisper that she's probably a lesbian, a tactic some members of the Women's Liberation Front have encountered. I am not anti-male any more than I am anti-white, and I am not anti-white, because I understand that white people, like black ones, are victims of a racist society. They are products of their time and place. It's the same with men. This society is as anti-woman as it is anti-black. It has forced males to adopt discriminatory attitudes toward females. Getting rid of them will be very hard for most men—too hard, for many of them.

Women are challenged now as never before. Their numbers in public office, in the professions, and in other key fields are declining, not increasing. The decline has been gradual and steady for the last twenty years. It will be difficult to reverse at first. The women who undertake to do it will be stigmatized as "odd" and "unfeminine" and must be prepared to endure such punishment. Eventually the point will be made that women are not different from men in their intelligence and ability and that women who aspire to important jobs—president of the company, member of Congress, and so on—are not odd and unfeminine. They aspire for the same reasons as any man—they think they can do the job and they want to try.

For years to come, most men will jeer at the women's liberation groups that are springing up. But they will someday realize that countless women, including their own wives and especially their daughters, silently applaud the liberation groups and share their goals, even if they are unable to bring themselves to rebel openly. American women are beginning to respond to our oppression. While most of us are not yet revolutionaries, the time is coming when we will be. The world must be taught that, to use the words of Women's Liberation activist Robin Morgan, "Women are not inherently passive or peaceful. We're not inherently anything but human. And like every other oppressed people rising up today, we're out for our freedom by any means necessary."

LITERACY: DEMOCRACY'S BASIC INGREDIENT

ADULT LITERACY AND BASIC EDUCATION
VOLUME 12, NUMBER 2 (1988)
BY SHIRLEY CHISHOLM

NOTE: The Honorable Shirley Chisholm is the first Black woman to be elected to the Congress of the United States and is the first Black woman to seek the US presidency. She has a distinguished record of fighting for human equality and social justice. This article was the closing address at the 1988 Commission on Adult Basic Education Conference in Seattle.

Abstract
In her fight for social justice, the Honorable Shirley Chisholm has met and talked with people throughout the United States. In this keynote address to the Commission on Adult Basic Education Conference, she concludes that literacy skills are a basic ingredient critical to the survival of a democratic society. Reading is discussed as an empowerment tool for

allowing all people to freely participate in the democratic process. The dangers of illiteracy are pointed out. Recognizing that knowledge is power, Chisholm stresses the relationship of the educational and political establishment to a literate society and the relationship between literacy and social equality.

Introduction
Distinguished members of the education profession, I consider it a privilege, an opportunity, and in a certain sense an obligation to be able to make a presentation to you. Because I have had the added opportunity of being able to travel around this country five times during the past 25 years of my life, I have also been able to meet with and talk with persons who have a deep abiding interest in the most important resources that any nation ever has—its young. I have had the opportunity to participate in several kinds of educational conferences, to visit in many schools across this nation, and to talk to parents in the North, the South, the East, and the West. I also have had the opportunity to go out in the villages, the towns, and the cities to talk to the little folk out there and to receive from them what they feel are some of the problems, some of the concerns, and some of the things they would really like to see done. But because of the fact that they are merely laypersons, they have not always had the opportunity to make the kinds of contributions that are so terribly important. Based on this background, I am going to share some thoughts on power and illiteracy in this country. I do not expect that you will necessarily agree with everything I say or with everything that I do. The important thing is for me to be honest and forthright in the hope that at least I may provoke your thinking because we have to be able to learn to accept constructive criticism.

The Need for Reading Skills
A democratic society depends upon the intelligence and the wisdom of the mass of the people to keep it moving. A government of the people, by the people, and for the people necessarily depends upon the people's judgment to help to make decisions that will affect their lives. If the people are not able to read, to communicate, and to comprehend, an atmosphere is likely to develop in a multifaceted, multicultural society such as ours where dormant hostilities and frustration rise to the breaking point and where sanity and reason are pushed to the back burner giving way to strident voices and sometimes uncontrolled emotions.

Reading skills are tantamount to a degree of success in today's world. In a highly automated and technological society, you are unable to function effectively without the ability to read and understand what has been read. If you are not able to read job applications and travel directions, and such things as maps and time tables, you can never be able to develop confidence in yourself. How can you become an effective citizen in a democracy unless you are able to read the facts, to digest them, to have the opportunity to engage in intelligent conversations and discussions, to be able to debate the pros and the cons, and to expand that great resource of the human mind to become more enlightened and knowledgeable with respect to the very complex society in which you live? How can you use the ballot box if you cannot read the newspapers, the referendums, and the political literature in order to be cognizant of the issues? Reading is almost synonymous with knowledge, and knowledge is power. Power is the mechanism used by the body politic to translate man's needs and desires into meaningful and relevant kinds of programs that will help to bring about ultimately and inevitably the amelioration of the human condition. If you are not able to read, then your life is ultimately controlled for you by others who interpret and translate for you.

The Basic Ingredient

You all know that phrase of "education is the key." Reading is the basic ingredient in the educational process because it determines to a very large extent how far one will be able to rise in America. The individual is not able to develop life-fulfilling answers without the most basic tools for personal advancement. How can the experiences of life lead to the best decisions about work and family development if the individual is an adult with the responsibilities of adulthood but without the most basic tools for successful plain day-to-day living—the ability to read, to comprehend, and to write with some ease? If adults have severe reading problems, it is easy to see the correlation between low literacy and unemployment. If nonreading adults are less likely to exercise their right to vote, it is easy to understand why the low literate members of the community are politically powerless and are seldom listened to in the center of decision making. In the words of a 1965 report, "adult illiteracy is among those powerful and tragic influences that spawn the ills of the central city. The illiterate adult faces a high probability of sustained unemployment even in the face of labor shortages in skilled and technical occupations." This adult cannot offer example, inspiration, hope, stability, or even family security because talents and potential productive capacity are imprisoned in a human being without a key to personal betterment.

Ignorance is poverty. Ignorance is disease. Ignorance is unemployment and isolation. Ignorance, believe it or not, is also an opportunity for the exploitation of the many by the few. I have seen it. Ignorance stampedes people into the acceptance of simple answers which are nearly always the wrong answers. If knowledge truly is power, then ignorance truly is weakness. No country, no society, or no family can really flourish in weakness.

Employers and businesses know better than the rest of us how unready so many of our graduates nowadays are for the work world. Much basic remedial education is needed. An article recently in *Business Week* magazine revealed the magnitude of the functional illiteracy problem. One example was an insurance company clerk who did not understand decimal points and issued a claims check for $2,200 instead of the authorized amount of $22.00. In another example, a CBS teleprompter who could not read caused TV correspondent Fred Graham to sound like he was stuttering when the machine lagged behind his rate of speech.

The United States Department of Education estimates that one in seven Americans, 25 million adults, cannot read or even compute at a sixth-grade level. Over 2 million more people join these ranks each year in the greatest democracy on the face of this planet called Earth. Obviously this is not a problem of the kind of knowledge being conveyed; this is really no knowledge at all getting through. But even for people who are not functionally illiterate, many are not prepared by many of our schools for lives as workers, as consumers, as voters, or even as parents in the coming years. Is knowledge being equally spread across this country? Is the same opportunity to gain knowledge available to students who are Black, who are Native American, who are Hispanics, who live in blighted urban neighborhoods or travel with their families throughout this country during the different seasons picking the vegetables and the fruits that people enjoy in the large urban centers, or who have physical handicaps? You have probably guessed my answer to the question because so much of my own career has been spent fighting for equality of educational opportunities. Still, there is no question that the quality of education is yet unequal across the land. I have seen it recently in my trips around this nation.

Empowerment Through Reading

Yet, all of us know as educators that reading is the key to competence and security. For if an individual lacks the competency to secure a job, then it naturally follows that life is insecure at best in today's world. This person certainly will not be able to satisfy basic economic and social needs. In other words, cultural, social, and political advancement is virtually impossible as we advance into the 21st century without the ability to read. National statistics indicate that 46% of the adults who have had some high school but have not completed high school account for 64% of the unemployment force. Over 60% of jobless fathers receiving aid to dependent children have no education beyond the elementary school level. A teacher and a friend of mine who is an assistant professor at the city university has said that education in contemporary society is concerned not only with literacy and skills per se but also with actions and values. An active society is one that is master of itself. You cannot be master of yourself unless you are literate. Such control allows you to respond to changing situations and to transform yourself. You understand that social laws can be altered. An active society presents an inherently secular vision of humankind in that by definition actors are consciously capable of changing their social combinations, changing themselves, and in effect becoming the creators of their own lives. Active individuals and literate individuals are aware of their identities and of who they are and what they must be about. They possess the ability to act, and they seek to control their own lives. Therefore, we know that knowledge and information become the crucial variables for both the active society and the active individual. But both must have knowledge and information to act, to transform, to create, and to recognize the limitations of their actions and beliefs in order to make the necessary changes in their lives and their social reality.

The Dangers of Illiteracy

All of us have to face this reality, and sometimes we would rather push the proverbial problems under the proverbial rug. It is easier to do that, but we do have to face reality. The reality is that a disproportionate number of Americans are unable to function in today's modern world due to illiteracy. This low-literate population in any community continues to be unemployed and underemployed and continues to be poor. Thus, there is no legacy to bequeath to future generations to come. So actually in realistic terms, we may be perpetuating a society that is not even going to be able to get out of the problems that confront it. This segment of the society of course then is likely to be and is excluded from access to the influential centers of government, commerce, and the media. No powerful political base can emerge with a large number of low illiterates. Their development will come about as a result of the effectiveness of coalitions formed by the various segments in the community because after all that is the bottom line. Business has a vested interest in lower unemployment and in reduced crime. Greater literacy amongst the adults will help in all of these areas, and business must be made a very important part of this coalition of which I speak. They must be educated to this fact because ultimately if the citizens in the various communities of the cities, the villages, and the town across this nation are not literate, then it means that the businesses in the community cannot succeed or develop. So there is a wonderful kind of intertwining.

Inevitably, if people are not educated in America as we proceed into the 21st century, Japan, West Germany, and many other countries are going to surpass us. Indeed, they are doing so right now in several areas. We should have a very definite concern about what all this really means. How are we going to translate these problems that confront us in our educational centers without becoming defensive every time someone offers constructive criticism? When we look at what is happening around the world in terms of its impact on us in the United States of America, we have to recognize that we are losing our positions very fast in terms of our place in this world.

The educational establishment has a vested interest in having parents in a position to be able to help their children to learn in schools. I just came back from Tennessee and Arkansas. I was so excited at what I saw in some of the schools in the educational systems in those two states. Here they had classes twice a week from 7 to 9 in the evening to help the parents in the school districts to help their children in terms of the school curriculum and the understanding of what the educational establishment was trying to do. I sat in on a couple of these classes and was so rekindled, reinvigorated, and re-energized as I saw the beautiful relationship developing amongst the teachers and the parents. The parents were not afraid to ask questions because of the potential embarrassment they might feel if they were not able to handle the English language correctly. This was because the teachers and administrators in these particular situations had indicated not through their rhetoric but through their patterns of behavior that we are here to help each other and the children for which both of us have a responsibility. You as the educator and I as the parent cannot really succeed in preparing these children for the future century unless we work together. It was a beautiful thing!

I spoke with some of the parents. They say, "It is just so wonderful; I feel a little bit more secure; I feel better because the teachers are so wonderful and they don't make us embarrassed. We ask questions and they show us." We don't always have to depend on the curriculum as such. We don't always have to depend on the workbook as such. Some of us become so doctrinaire and inflexible that we forget that we must be able to visualize and to understand the persons that we are attempting to improve in the society.

In a sense, adult educators are part of the talented group in the United States of America who had the opportunity to be formally educated and to be able to utilize that education in a way that can help other people who have not had that opportunity. There is absolutely no reason, no reason at all as far as I am concerned, for the richest nation in the world to have a population where approximately 26 million of its adults are functionally illiterate. It is a blot on this country which claims to give to every man, women, and child equality of opportunity for them to rise to their fullest potential. Rhetoric must be replaced by action, and I know that so many of you wonderful people in the area of adult illiteracy are already replacing rhetoric with action. For that I congratulate you from the depths of my heart. As the saying in the street goes, "You know where it is at."

Knowledge is power, but without a literate population the ability to use power for the amelioration of the human condition is meaningless. Francis Bacon, the great Englishman who in 1597 coined the phrase "Knowledge is Power," certainly was not writing a battle-field strategy. Two years earlier in 1595, Bacon wrote that the monuments of wit always survive the monuments of power. He knew as people since have too often forgotten that the power of thought and ideas inevitably triumphs over the transitory and illusionary power of weaponry. But I am not here to rail against the madness of militarism; that is another speech for another day. Surely, each of us can imagine the Garden of Eden that this world could be if weapons and war would disappear and all of resources were turned to eradicating every source of misery including a modern day misery that confronts us at this very moment in America. That misery is illiteracy. The nurturing and spreading of knowledge in this country needs far greater thought and attention if indeed the needs of all Americans are to be met.

Our leaders have a responsibility to build and to encourage the public knowledge from which their power derives. They in turn must be made responsible for using that power that we give to them for the best interest of the people in this democratic society. But clearly to me, the burden of responsibility does not rest solely on our elected representatives because the principle that knowledge is power applies to every one of us in every aspect of our lives because politically we can know how best to make the system work to our advantage. In our jobs, we can know how best to perform and advance to higher positions because of this knowledge we have. Financially we can know how best to budget and invest our hard-earned money. In our relations with our family and our friends, we can know how to best please the ones we love and in turn benefit from their affection.

But illiteracy diminishes the benefits that can be derived from a democratic society. Ours is an open system of government which relies upon knowledge. From the first patriots to the founders of universal free public education to the defenders of the freedom of press in this nation, we have had an unbending heritage of knowledge which is supposed to be shared widely and without restraint. We have to remain vigilant and strong against proponents of ignorance and secrecy—against those who would hold the knowledge back from the American people for whatever reason of discrimination, self-advancement, ideology, or even fear of retribution. The times when knowledge was withheld as when the truth about the war in Vietnam was hidden from the public are times of blight and tragedy on our national record. Illiteracy is also a time of blight and tragedy on our national record today.

Finally, humanity's search and mankind's hunger for knowledge continues to persist just as this search and hunger must have had some concern among the primitive people who were tired of waiting for lightning to light their fires. Fresh knowledge still lights new roads for ourselves and for our civilization in this automated and technological age. Thus, there is absolutely no room for illiteracy because illiteracy impedes progress. Illiteracy stifles development. Illiteracy frustrates the mind. Illiteracy curtains initiative. Illiteracy destroys the creative spark in our human soul. Illiteracy fosters pretensive behavior due to societal embarrassment. Finally, illiteracy lulls the individual into a physical or psychological inferiority syndrome which deadens the motivation for developing the individual's fullest potential.

In closing, as we begin to move towards the 21st century, the time has come to reaffirm the commitment not only to the lifting of illiterate folks as we climb but also to the concept of equity as well. The time has come to declare that America's greatest asset is not her weapons but her people and that we are cognizant of the fact that only the fittest will survive. The time has come to consider education not a cost but an investment in the future. The time has come to reaffirm that our greatest hope is not the technology of Star Wars but the eradication of illiteracy in America. This nation is great because ultimately we believe in our people. I believe that we do. We believe in our people, and we must be able to reject the utterance of someone who said that human beings start out as butterflies and end up as cocoons. As my good friend, who is the president of Barnard College in the city of New York said just the other day at a commencement "Education is empowerment—individual and national empowerment. For the United States of America to be populated by a citizenry that is uneducated is a prescription for disaster and a sentence to everlasting continual persistent mediocrity."

SHIRLEY CHISHOLM ANNOUNCES HER CANDIDACY FOR THE US PRESIDENCY

January 25, 1972

I stand before you today as a candidate for the Democratic nomination for the Presidency of the United States of America.

I am not the candidate of black America, although I am black and proud.

I am not the candidate of the women's movement of this country, although I am a woman, and I am equally proud of that.

I am not the candidate of any political bosses or fat cats or special interests.

I stand here now without endorsements from many big name politicians or celebrities or any other kind of prop. I do not intend to offer to you the tired and glib clichés, which for too long have been an accepted part of our political life. I am the candidate of the people of America. And my presence before you now symbolizes a new era in American political history.

I have always earnestly believed in the great potential of America. Our constitutional democracy will soon celebrate its 200th anniversary, effective testimony, to the longevity to our cherished constitution and its unique bill of rights, which continues to give to the world an inspirational message of freedom and liberty.

We Americans are a dynamic people.

Fellow Americans, we have looked in vain to the Nixon administration for the courage, the spirit, the character and the words to lift us. To bring out the best in us, to rekindle in each of us our faith in the American dream. Yet all we have received in return is just another smooth exercise in political manipulation, deceit and deception, callousness and indifference to our individual problems and a disgusting playing of devices politics. Pinning the young against the old, labor against management, north against south, black against white. The abiding concern of this administration has been one of political expediency, rather than the needs of man's nature.

The president has broken his promises to us, and has therefore lost his claim to our trust and confidence in him. I cannot believe that this administration would ever have been elected four years ago, if we had known then what we know today. But we are entering a new era, in which we must, as Americans, must demand stature and size in our leadership—leadership, which is fresh, leadership, which is open, and leadership, which is receptive to the problems of all Americans.

I have faith in the American people. I believe that we are smart enough to correct our mistakes. I believe that we are intelligent enough to recognize the talent, energy, and dedication, which all Americans including women and minorities have to offer. I know from my travels to the cities and small towns of America that we have a vast potential, which can and must be put to constructive use in getting this great nation together. I know that millions of Americans, from all walks of life agree with me that leadership does not mean putting the ear to the ground, to follow public opinion, but to have the vision of what is necessary and the courage to make it possible, building a strong and just society, which in its diversity and is noble in its quality of life.

I stand before you today, to repudiate the ridiculous notion that the American people will not vote for qualified candidates, simply because he is not white or because she is not a male. I do not believe that in 1972, the great majority of Americans will continue to harbor such narrow and petty prejudice.

I am convinced that the American people are in a mood to discard the politics and political personalities of the past.

I believe that they will show in 1972, and thereafter, that they intend to make individual judgments on the merits of a particular candidate, based on that candidate's intelligence, character, physical ability, competence, integrity, and honesty." Clapping. "It is, I feel the duty of responsible leaders in this country to encourage and maximize, not to dismiss and minimize such judgment.

Americans all over are demanding a new sensibility, a new philosophy of government from Washington. Instead of sending spies to snoop on participants on Earth Day, I would welcome the efforts of concerned citizens of all ages to stop the abuse of our environment. Instead of watching a football game on television, while young people beg for the attention of their President, concerning our actions abroad, I would encourage them to speak out, organize for peaceful change, and vote in November. Instead of blocking efforts to control huge amounts of money given political candidates by the rich and the powerful, I would provide certain limits on such amounts and encourage all people of this nation to contribute small sums to the candidates of their choice. Instead of calculating political cost of this or that policy, and of weighing in favors of this or that group, depending on whether that group voted for me in 1968, I would remind all Americans at this hour of the words of Abraham Lincoln, "A house divided cannot stand."

We Americans are all fellow countrymen. One day confronting the judgment of history in our country. We are all God's children and a bit of each of us is as precious as the will of the most powerful general or corporate millionaire. Our will can create a new America in 1972, one where there is freedom from violence and war, at home and abroad, where there is freedom from poverty and discrimination, where there exists at least a feeling, that we are making progress and assuring for everyone medical care, employment, and decent housing. Where we more decisively clean up our streets, our water, and our air. Where we work together, black and white, to rebuild our neighborhoods and to make our cities quiet, attractive, and efficient and fundamentally where we live in the confidence that every man and every woman in America has at long last the opportunity to become all that he was created of being, such as his ability.

In conclusion, all of you who share this vision, from New York to California, from Wisconsin to Florida, are brothers and sisters on the road to national unity and a new America. Those of you who were locked outside of the convention hall in 1968, those of you who can now vote for the first time, those of you who agree with me that the institutions of this country belong to all of the people who inhabit it. Those of you who have been neglected, left out, ignored, forgotten, or shunted aside for whatever reason, give me your help at this hour. Join me in an effort to reshape our society and regain control of our destiny as we go down the Chisholm Trail for 1972.

US POLICY AND BLACK REFUGEES

THE HONORABLE SHIRLEY CHISHOLM (D-NY)
ISSUE: A JOURNAL OF OPINION 12., NOS. 1–2 (1982): 22–24.

NOTE: This is the text of an address delivered to a symposium titled "Africa and Caribbean Refugees" at the Twenty-Fifth Annual Meeting of the African Studies Association, November 6, 1982, Washington, DC.

The debate over who is a "legitimate refugee" involves more than just a quarrel over definitions. Haitians and African refugees, largely Ethiopians, have come to our shores in much the same manner as previous groups. The reaction to the arrival of these groups, however, must be seen in the context of legal and political changes in American society.

The "first asylum" phenomenon of persons fleeing to the United States as their first place of refuge from persecution has become the primary focus of any policy decisions affecting our refugee and immigration laws. Further, the "first asylum" issue has blurred the distinctions between refugees and immigrants. The controversy surrounding the "first asylum" issue emanates from two areas: our foreign policy in the Western Hemisphere is based on the perception that "first asylees" flee to the U.S. for economic reasons rather than a "well-founded fear of persecution on the basis of race, religion, political opinion or membership in a social group," the definition for a refugee and/or asylee as embodied in the Refugee Act of 1980. Secondly, the new "asylees" are overwhelmingly persons of color in comparison to earlier immigrant groups which were largely European.

First, the majority of the people fleeing to this country as "first asylees" come from Western Hemispheric countries like El Salvador, Haiti, and most recently Guatemala. These countries are not simply allies to the United States—their governments receive a substantial amount of military and/or economic assistance from us. In addition, the Reagan Administration has made it quite clear that it will support the existing governments in such countries against any revolutionary or liberating forces. Needless to say, this support often contributes to refugee flight from the Caribbean and Central American nations.

Secondly, the poor economic conditions in countries like Haiti provide an easy excuse for labeling Haitians as "economic refugees." This characterization, of course, ignores the political conditions in the home country and encourages the presumption that nationals from Haiti are fleeing to the United States solely for economic reasons.

The color question overlays the politics of our refugee policies. Clare Booth Luce, who serves on the President's Foreign Intelligence Advisory Board, was recently chastised for her remarks in the September issue of *Geo* magazine where she suggested that America's new immigrants were a threat to American culture. Her remarks are worth repeating here: "In the Nineteenth Century, the United States absorbed something like forty million immigrants. But the vast majorities were of a fundamental culture, and they were all white. They were not black or brown or yellow."

Luce's statement, while perhaps embarrassing to the administration, is indicative of the thoughts behind some of the administration's policy formulations. Refugees, who are people of color, are assumed to be incapable of integrating into American society. Ms. Luce forgot that black Americans preceded 19th century European immigrants and that our society is not *white* but rather multi-cultural. That is why jazz remains America's only original art form despite efforts to make square-dancing the official American national dance.

The marked increase in numbers of "first asylum" cases has certainly heightened the debate in this area. In 1980, 125,000 Cubans came to South Florida in the mariel exodus. Notably, *these* Cubans were of a darker hue than their predecessors in the 1960s. During this same year, it is estimated that 12,000 Haitians arrived on U.S. shores. Over 100,000 Salvadorans entered the United States in 1981. This level of mass asylum is a new concept for U.S. immigration and refugee law. The genesis of the current crisis results from the fact that when Congress adopted the Refugee Act of 1980, the Act was silent on the issue of the United States as a country of first asylum. Needless to say, the mariel exodus and the continuing flow of Haitian and Salvadoran refugees focused attention on this first asylum issue very quickly.

The next question, of course, is how have we responded as a country of first asylum. As signatories to the U.N. protocol relating to refugees in 1968, the U.S. has certain international obligations toward refugees who are defined as persons who have a "well-founded fear of being persecuted for reasons of race, religion, nationality, membership in the particular social group, or political opinion." Our own refugee laws, as a result of the Refugee Act of 1980, largely incorporate this definition. Of special significance is the protocol's prohibition of the deportation of a refugee "to the frontiers of territories where his life or freedom would be threatened. . . ." It also requires that its provisions be applied "without discrimination as to race, religion or country of origin." Our problems with "first asylum" issues largely stem from our inability to accept this definition with "political" qualifications. As a country, the U.S. has been far more interested in responding to refugee concerns when we gained some political benefit than in addressing humanitarian need. In fact, only in the case of Cubans, and to a lesser extent Nicaraguans, has the U.S. responded positively to its obligations as country of first asylum. In both cases, we perceived that it was in our political interest to accept Cubans as refugees and to grant extended voluntary departure status to Nicaraguans. For example, Haitian political prisoners, who were released from prison through the intervention of U.N. Ambassador Andrew Young, were dissuaded by our own state department officials from applying for political asylum in the United States. In this instance, we obviously saw no political gains from accepting Haitians as political prisoners. Geo-political considerations reveal far more about why we have pre-judged Haitian asylum claims as frivolous and rejected Salvadorans as refugees than any other explanation. These considerations raise the question generally of whether we have equal application of our refugee laws or differential treatment. Let me cite a few examples.

New York City papers recently carried the story of four Polish nationals who arrived in Elizabeth, New Jersey. They were granted asylum after only six days in the Brooklyn Detention Center and released. Yet Haitian nationals waited over a year before their release from the Detention Center. Two small boats of Cuban refugees have landed in Miami within the last two weeks. The Cubans have immediately been released to their family members while Haitians, with family members in the area, were denied release from the Krome Detention Camp until very recently.

These comparisons only confirm a continuing racial and ideological bias in our refugee and asylum law. Despite a change in our immigration laws to accommodate the U.N. definition of a refugee, we still respond more favorably to those persons fleeing from a communist regime. For example, from January 1974 to May 1975, none of the Filipinos or South Koreans who requested asylum were granted it. The State Department also recommended that asylum requests be denied to sixteen Greeks who sought political refuge before the fall of the Junta, and to the eight South Vietnamese who asked asylum from the Thieu regime. Yet during this same period, scarcely any requests from Eastern European countries were denied. Between 1975 and 1976, the last year for which data is available, 96 percent of the applicants fleeing rightist governments were denied refuge in the United States, while 95 percent of those applicants from communist countries, in the same time period, were granted sanctuary here. In the particular case of Haitian boat people arriving in Florida and requesting asylum eighteen have been granted asylum, less than one percent of the total.

In spite of a humanitarian change in the United States refugee law in 1980, which eliminated any legal basis for discriminating in favor of those fleeing communist countries, fully 95 percent of those whom the United States has admitted as refugees since the change still come from communist countries in Southeast Asia, Eastern Europe, or the Soviet Union. Furthermore, the quick action on the asylum claims of the four Poles, while Haitians forcibly exiled from Haiti in November 1980 have yet to receive a ruling on their requests for asylum, illustrates the priority given to asylum claimants from communist countries.

Yet, the racial issue cannot be ignored here. The plight of Ethiopian nationals in this country is a clear example of the racism inherent in our policies. The State Department's decision to revoke the extended voluntary departure status granted to Ethiopians in August of 1981 was greeted with cries of racism. At the same time that we were granting this status to Poles, the State Department was removing this status for Ethiopians. Here, we have a people who fled a communist-ruled government just like Poland or other Eastern European countries. Yet, they received decidedly different treatment. Skin color is the only differential which explains this policy decision. Fortunately, through the efforts of Congressmen Jack Kemp (R-NY) and Julian Dixon (DCA), this decision was reversed.

Generally, our policy toward African refugees has been one of conflicting interests and benign neglect. Despite the presence of 25 percent of the world's refugee population in Africa, our annual admission quotas remain at the low level of 3000. When challenged on the small numbers, the State Department's defense is three-fold:

1. Africa takes care of its own and there is no need for permanent resettlement in the U.S.;
2. Africans are largely rural people and would not adjust well to American society; and
3. The U.S. compensates for these small numbers by giving economic assistance to refugees in Africa.

Such defenses are only a polite way of saying that African refugees are not a priority. While Africa's response to refugees is nothing short of remarkable, given her resources, many Africans could benefit from resettlement in the United States. The rural argument ignores the fact that Hmong Tribesmen were actively encouraged to apply for refugee admission to the U.S.; in this instance, a rural lifestyle in Indochina was no barrier for U.S. policy-makers. Finally, economic assistance from the U.S. is tenuous at best. Recently, the African Refugee Section, at State, estimated that the U.S. might withhold as much as $25 million in food aid that it pledged at the Geneva Conference on African Refugees in April of 1981. "Unforeseen donations by other countries, carry-overs . . . from previous years and reduced estimates" of refugee numbers prompted this change. It seems that even in terms of food aid, Africans receive second-class treatment.

Finally, we cannot ignore the feelings of the U.N. high commissioner for refugees and African leaders that the U.S. program encourages a "brain drain" from Africa. Individual liberty and choice, however, should not be sacrificed for the sake of governments' prestige. As long as the U.S. maintains a refugee program, Africans and other black refugees must be treated equitably.

Remarkably, these statistics and facts are not the worst aspects of our policies toward black refugees. Legal protection for refugees has been deliberately undermined by the Reagan Administration. The success of the Haitian lawsuits has generated a lot of discussion about eliminating federal court jurisdiction over asylum claims to prevent any future cases like *Haitian Refugee Center v. Civiletti*. These changes in court jurisdiction, of course, are being proposed in the guise of "streamlining the process." The real motive here, however, is to cut Haitians' access to the courts. This action is in direct response to the success of the Center's lawsuit and other lawsuits brought on behalf of Haitian asylum claimants.

The new immigration reform package, the Simpson-Mazzoli Bill, severely restricts judicial review of asylum claims. The bill punishes the victims of discriminatory policies for successfully using our legal system to thwart those policies. This action is not "streamlining the process" for efficiency but rather a blatant drive to cut aliens' access to our courts.

The policy of interdiction is a clear violation of the U.S.'s responsibility for the protection of refugees. Without specific legislative authority, the Coast Guard has interdicted three boats carrying Haitian nationals and returned these people back to Haiti. There is no definitive information about the fate of these returnees. Interdiction has certainly eliminated most of the Haitian boat traffic but one must ask at what cost in terms of resources and people.

Perhaps the most heinous policy of the Reagan Administration has been the imprisonment of Haitians for the past year. With the exception of the detention of Japanese-Americans during World War II, no other group has been treated so inhumanely. Over 2,000 Haitian asylum seekers were dispersed in twelve different facilities around the country, including Puerto Rico. At least three deaths occurred during the year-long detention. In addition, federal prisons were used to detain Haitians who had been accused of no crime either in the United States or in Haiti. The racist treatment of Haitians is clear; no other group has been placed in our federal prisons without first being labeled as a criminal.

One must also be mindful of the forced repatriation of refugees processed for admission to the U.S. in Djibouti and the recent debacle with Ethiopians on extended voluntary departure in the U.S. As with Civil Rights issues generally, Human Rights advocates must expect deliberate attempts by this administration to obfuscate its international commitments to refugees when it is politically expedient.

As scholars interested in the peoples of the African Diaspora, we have a responsibility to monitor and influence foreign policies which impact the Caribbean and Africa. Certainly, the plight of black refugees in this country is an issue to which we must all respond. Refugee policy is an adjunct of our broader foreign policy goals. Since U.S. foreign policy is greatly determined by ethnic pressure, it is imperative that black Americans become intimately involved in shaping American foreign policy, including refugee policy. State Department reaction to Polish Martial Law, the Turkish invasion of Cyprus, and the Israeli attacks in Lebanon, greatly shaped America's policies in these situations. We must not be tempted by those who use immigrants and refugees as scapegoats for the economic plight of black Americans. We must be willing to advocate for the protection of black refugees now; otherwise, we will be at a distinct disadvantage when the crisis in South Africa reaches its climax, as it surely will in the near future.

STUDY QUESTIONS

1. Shirley Chisholm was a feminist. Based upon the primary sources, what were the pressing issues facing women in 1970? To what extent have women made progress in the twenty-first century?
2. Based on the original sources and the material in the book, why and how does Chisholm connect issues of poverty and race to support a woman's right to abortion and contraception?
3. Chisholm's 1972 presidential has been described as both pathbreaking and quixotic. Why did Chisholm wish to run for the presidency? What did Chisholm believe were the most compelling issues facing the American people?
4. Chisholm always saw herself as a teacher. How did Chisholm campaign for public education and expand access to higher education?
5. How did Chisholm challenge the racial nature of the US policy on immigration? Have there been significant changes since 1980?

NOTES

INTRODUCTION

1. Anita Hill, interview, Shirley Chisholm Papers Archive (hereafter cited as SCPA), November 27, 2011; Shirley Chisholm, *The Good Fight,* 152–153.

CHAPTER 1: BARBADOS

1. Ronald Tree, *A History of Barbados,* 60.
2. Muriel Forde interview, Shola Lynch Collection, SCPA, 11.
3. Paule Marshall, *Triangular Road: A Memoir,* 67.
4. Forde interview, SCPA, 6.
5. Shirley Chisholm, *Unbought and Unbossed,* 25.
6. *New York Times,* June 25, 1972, 13.
7. Gloria Steinem presentation on Shirley Chisholm, SCPA, November 2008, 14.

CHAPTER 2: BROOKLYN

1. Chisholm, *Unbought and Unbossed,* 31.
2. Craig Wilder, *A Covenant with Color: Race and Social Power in Brooklyn,* 180.
3. Chisholm, *Unbought and Unbossed,* 30.
4. Ibid., 35.
5. Ibid., 36.
6. Ibid., 33.
7. *New York Times,* April 7, 1895.
8. Chisholm, *Unbought and Unbossed,* 39.
9. Ibid., 42.
10. Ibid., 43.

CHAPTER 3: ALL POLITICS IS LOCAL

1. James Haskins, *Fighting Shirley Chisholm,* 65.
2. Interview with Shirley Chisholm, New York, 1968, Audio C-160, Part VII, Schomburg Library.
3. Chisholm, *Unbought and Unbossed,* 63.
4. Basil Paterson interview, SCPA.

CHAPTER 4: BLACK POWER

1. Interview with Donald Maggin, May 20, 2012, SCPA.
2. Marcus Garvey quoted in Brian Purnell, "Revolution Has Come to Brooklyn," in *Black Power at Work: Community Control, Affirmative Action, and the Construction Industry*, edited by David Goldberg and Trevor Griffey, 38.
3. Shirley Chisholm, interview, New York, 1968, sc Audio C-161, pt. XIV, Schomburg Center; Jocelyn Cooper quoted in Julie Gallagher, "Women of Action in Action: The New Politics of Black Women in New York City, 1944–1972," 162; Ruth Goring quoted in Carlos Russell, unpublished manuscript, Schomburg Center, 160.
4. Chisholm, *Unbought and Unbossed*, 66, 68–69.
5. Russell, unpublished manuscript, 166.
6. Chisholm, *Unbought and Unbossed*, 77.
7. Ibid.; Chisholm, interview, New York, 1968, sc Audio C-161.
8. Quoted in Gallagher, "Women of Action in Action," 171.

CHAPTER 5: NEW YORK STATE ASSEMBLYWOMAN

1. Chisholm, *Unbought and Unbossed*, 76–77.
2. Susan Brownmiller, "This Is Fighting Shirley Chisholm," 34.
3. Ibid.
4. Ibid.
5. Chisholm, *Unbought and Unbossed*, 78.
6. Brownmiller, "This Is Fighting Shirley Chisholm," 34.
7. Chisholm interview, #161, side 1, no. 1, Schomburg Center.
8. Ibid.

CHAPTER 6: I AM WOMAN

1. The Miss America protest was not the first women's liberation demonstration against the sexual exploitation of women. In May 1968, Seattle Radical Women disrupted a University of Washington Men's Commission event that brought a Playboy bunny to the campus. I was in the demonstration. See Barbara Winslow, "Primary and Secondary Contradictions in Seattle, 1967–69," in *The Feminist Memoir Project*.
2. Jitu Weusi, interview, SCPA.
3. As quoted in Brownmiller, "This Is Fighting Shirley Chisholm," 87.
4. As quoted in Gallagher, "Women of Action in Action," 178.
5. Chisholm *Unbought and Unbossed*, 83.
6. Brownmiller, "This Is Fighting Shirley Chisholm," 85.
7. Ibid., 83.
8. Basil Paterson, interview, SCPA.
9. Josh Guild, "To Make That Someday Come: Shirley Chisholm's Radical Politics of Possibility," 254.
10. Chisholm interview, #161, side 1, no. 1, Schomburg Center.
11. Chisholm, *Unbought and Unbossed*, 86.
12. Haskins, *Fighting Shirley Chisholm*, 127.
13. Gallagher, "Women of Action in Action," 104.
14. Haskins, *Fighting Shirley Chisholm*, 117.

15. Chisholm interview, #161, side 1, bo.1 Schomberg Center.

16. James Farmer, *Lay Bare the Heart: An Autobiography of the Civil Rights Movement*, 314.

CHAPTER 7: AN UNQUIET CONGRESSWOMAN

1. Chisholm, *Unbought and Unbossed*, 80.

2. Ibid., 152.

3. Ibid.

4. Susan Brownmiller, *Shirley Chisholm: A Biography*, 153.

5. Shola Lynch, documentary, *Chisholm '72: Unbought and Unbossed*.

6. Chisholm, *Unbought and Unbossed*, 106.

7. Ibid., 103.

8. Ibid., 112.

9. *New York Times*, May 22, 1970, 34.

10. US Congress, *Congressional Record*, 92nd Cong., 1st sess., March 30, 1971.

11. *McCall's*, August 1970, 41.

12. *It's About Time, Black Panther Party* newspaper, February 2, 1972 #20.

13. Phyllis Palmer, "Outside the Law," 431.

14. *McCall's*, August 1970, 41.

15. Eileen Shanahan, "Women Organize for Political Power," *New York Times*, July 11, 1971, 1.

16. Jeanne Theoharis, *The Rebellious Life of Mrs. Rosa Parks*, 218.

17. Chisholm, *Unbought and Unbossed*, 131.

18. As quoted in Gallagher, "Women of Action in Action," 179.

19. Chisholm, *Unbought and Unbossed*, 140.

CHAPTER 8: TESTING THE PRESIDENTIAL WATERS

1. *New York Times*, June 9, 1970, 33.

2. Ibid., November 1, 1970, 22.

3. Haskins, *Fighting Shirley Chisholm*, 149.

4. Brownmiller, *Shirley Chisholm: A Biography*, 139.

5. Chisholm, *Unbought and Unbossed*, 128.

6. Julie Gallagher, *Black Women and Politics in New York City*, 181.

7. Jo Freeman, "Mrs. Smith Runs for President," *Maine Sunday Telegram*, January 30, 2000, City Edition, C3.

8. Manning Marable, *Race, Reform, and Rebellion: The Second Reconstruction and Beyond in Black America*, 116.

9. Chisholm, *The Good Fight*, 29.

10. Ibid., 30–31.

11. *New York Times*, November 20, 1971.

12. James Richardson, *Willie Brown: A Biography*, 195.

13. *New York Times*, October 3, 1971.

14. Chisholm, *The Good Fight*, 34.

15. *New York Times*, January 30, 1972, 22.

16. Chisholm, *The Good Fight*, 51.

17. Carolyn Smith, interview, SCPA, 22–28.

18. Marable, *Race, Reform, and Rebellion,* 121.

19. *New York Times,* February 4.

20. Marion Humphrey, interview, SCPA, 10.

21. Ibid., 11.

CHAPTER 9: ON THE CHISHOLM TRAIL

1. See "Shirley Chisholm Announces Her Candidacy for the US Presidency."

2. Chisholm, *The Good Fight,* 3.

3. Mink was responsible for shepherding Title IX of the 1972 Educational Amendments Act through the House. Written to prohibit sex discrimination in federally assisted education programs, it had its biggest impact on women's participation in collegiate sports. In April 1972, Mink traveled to Paris with New York representative Bella Abzug to meet with Madam Nguyen Thi Binh, a negotiator for the North Vietnamese government. This generated a lot of criticism.

4. Chisholm, *The Good Fight,* 56. As for embarrassing one's own people, in 1981 Hastings was charged with accepting a $150,000 bribe in exchange for a lenient sentence and a return of seized assets for twenty-one counts of racketeering and perjury. In 1988 the Democratic-controlled US House of Representatives took up the case, and Hastings was impeached for bribery and perjury. He was then convicted in 1989 by the US Senate, becoming the sixth federal judge in the history of the United States to be removed from office by the Senate.

5. Jim Pitts, interview, SCPA.

6. Liz Cohen, interview, SCPA.

7. Haskins, *Fighting Shirley Chisholm,* 166–167.

8. Chisholm, *The Good Fight,* 59–69.

9. Ibid., 59.

10. Ibid., 69.

11. Gloria Steinem, interview, SCPA.

12. Jo Freeman has a wonderful online report on Chisholm's campaign: www.jofreeman.com/polhistory/chisholm.htm.

13. Cohen, interview, SCPA.

14. Mark Solomon, interview, SCPA, 22.

15. Pitts, interview, SCPA, 10.

16. Solomon, interview, SCPA, 14; Chisholm, *The Good Fight,* 84.

17. Chisholm, *The Good Fight,* 82.

18. Curwood's daughter, Anastasia Curwood, is writing a book on Shirley Chisholm; she is a Visiting Fellow at the James Weldon Johnson Institute at Emory University.

19. Chisholm, *The Good Fight,* 80.

20. Ibid., 92.

21. Ibid., 97.

22. FBI file, Shirley Chisholm, no. 453411-000.

23. Pamela Martinez, interview, SCPA.

24. Chisholm, *The Good Fight,* 107.

25. Pitts, interview, SCPA, 15–16.

26. Richardson, *Willie Brown: A Biography,* 197. Ironically, Brown's rhetoric did not go over in the convention's black caucus meeting that had just earlier voted to endorse Chisholm.

27. Chisholm, *The Good Fight,* 131.

28. Percy Sutton, "In Nomination for the Presidency, the Name of Shirley Chisholm."

29. Richardson, *Willie Brown: A Biography,* 210.

30. Chisholm, *The Good Fight,* 1.

31. Ibid., 3.

CHAPTER 10: POLITICAL AND PERSONAL TRANSFORMATIONS

1. Gail Collins, *When Everything Changed: The Amazing Journey of American Women from 1960 to the Present,* 252–253.

2. Haskins, *Fighting Shirley Chisholm,* 187.

3. *New York Times,* October 10, 1972.

4. Haskins, *Fighting Shirley Chisholm,* 192.

5. Marable, *Race, Reform, and Rebellion,* 129.

6. Wayne Barrett and Andrew Cooper, "Chisholm's Compromises: Politics and the Art of Self-Interest," *Village Voice,* October 30, 1978.

7. *Essence,* August 1982, 74.

8. Ibid.

9. *New York Times,* February 11, 1982, 2:11.

CHAPTER 11: CONCLUSION

1. *Valley Advocate,* March 2, 1983, A6.

2. *Northampton Daily News,* April 4, 1983.

3. Cecelia Hartsell, e-mails to author, September 9, 1912.

4. *Northampton Daily News,* April 4, 1983.

5. http://pelosi.house.gov/news/press-releases/2009/03/releases-March09-chisholm.shtml.

BIBLIOGRAPHY

NEWSPAPERS

Amsterdam News. 1945–1982.
Barbados Weekly Herald. 1928–1934.
New York Times. 1964–2005.

ORAL HISTORY

Oral History Interviews

Chisholm, Shirley. Schomburg Library Center for Research in Black Culture, Oral History Tape Collection, New York Public Library, New York City.

The Shirley Chisholm Archive, which is part of the Shirley Chisholm Project of Brooklyn Women's Activism, 1945–present. Oral history interviews and transcripts are housed in the Chisholm Project office, 2403 James Building, at Brooklyn College, or in the Brooklyn College Library, Brooklyn College, Brooklyn, New York. Oral histories as videos are put on the project's web page, http://chisholmproject.com.

Janus Adams
Martha Baker
Pauline Barfield
Wayne Barrett
Yvonne Braithwaite-Burke
Donna Brazile
Vinie Burrows
Lizabeth Cohen
David Dinkins
Hazel Dukes
Muriel Forde
Jill Franklin
Robert Gottlieb
Richard Green
Nadine Hack

William Howard
Marion Humphrey
Rhoda Jacobs
Donald Maggin
Pamela Martinez
Muriel Morrisey
Basil Paterson
James Pitts
Loretta Ross
Patricia Schroeder
Mark Solomon
Nick Stefanizzi
Gloria Steinem
Jitu Weusi

Video

http://wn.com/shirley_chisholm_men_in_my_political_career.
Lynch, Shola. *Chisholm '72: Unbought and Unbossed.*

OTHER SOURCES

Beckles, Hilary McD. *A History of Barbados: From Amerindian Settlement to Caribbean Single Market.* Cambridge: Cambridge University Press, 2009.

Biondi, Martha. *To Stand and Fight: The Struggle for Civil Rights in Postwar New York City.* Cambridge, MA: Harvard University Press, 2003.

Blackburn, Robin. *The Making of New World Slavery: From the Baroque to the Modern.* New York: Verso, 1997.

Brown, David V. C. "Political Awakening in Bridgetown: The Wickham O'Neale Years." In *Beyond the Bridge: Lectures Commemorating Bridgetown's 375th Anniversary,* edited by Woodville Marchall and Pedro Welch. Cave Hill, Barbados: Barbados Museum and Historical Societies and the Department of History and Philosophy at the University of the West Indies, 2005.

Brownmiller, Susan. *Shirley Chisholm: A Biography.* New York: Doubleday, 1970.

———. "This Is Fighting Shirley Chisholm." *New York Times Magazine,* April 13, 2003.

Chisholm, Shirley. *The Good Fight.* New York: Harper and Row, 1973.

———. *Unbought and Unbossed: Expanded 40th Anniversary Edition.* Scott Simpson, ed. Washington, DC: Take Root Media, 2010.

Collins, Gail. *When Everything Changed: The Amazing Journey of American Women from 1960 to the Present.* New York: Little Brown and Co., 2009.

Connolly, Harold X. *A Ghetto Grows in Brooklyn.* New York: New York University Press, 1977.

Coulton, Thomas Evans. *A City College in Action: Struggle and Achievement at Brooklyn College, 1930–1955.* New York: Harper, 1955.

Dublin, Thomas, and Meloday James. "How Did Feminism Contribute to the Transformation of Radical Theater in the United States, 1966–1983?" *Women and Social Movements in the United States, 1600–2000* 17, no. 1 (March 2013), http://asp6new.alexanderstreet.com/wam2.

Farmer, James. *Lay Bare the Heart: An Autobiography of the Civil Rights Movement.* New York: Arbor House, 1985.

Gallagher, Julie. *Black Women and Politics in New York City.* Urbana: University of Illinois Press, 2012.

———. "Women of Action in Action: The New Politics of Black Women in New York City, 1944–1972." PhD diss., University of Massachusetts, 2003.

Goldberg, David, and Trevor Griffey, eds. *Black Power at Work: Community Control, Affirmative Action, and the Construction Industry.* Ithaca, NY: ILR Press, 2010.

Guild, Joshua. "To Make That Someday Come: Shirley Chisholm's Radical Politics of Possibility." In *Want to Start a Revolution? Radical Women in the Black Freedom Struggle,* edited by Dayo F. Gore, Jeanne Theoharis, and Komozi Woodard. New York: New York University Press, 2009.

Haskins, James. *Fighting Shirley Chisholm.* New York: Dial Press, 1975.

Horowitz, Murray M. *Brooklyn College: The First Half Century.* New York: Brooklyn College Press, 1981.

Marable, Manning. *Race, Reform, and Rebellion: The Second Reconstruction and Beyond in Black America, 1945–2006, Third Edition.* Jackson: University of Mississippi Press, 2007.

Marshall, Paule. *Brown Girl, Brownstones.* New York: Random House, 1959.

———. *Triangular Road: A Memoir.* New York: BasicCivitas Books, 2009.

Palmer, Phyllis. "Outside the Law: Agricultural and Domestic Workers Under the Fair Labor Standards Act." *Journal of Policy History* 7, no. 4 (October 1995), 416–440.

Purnell, Brian. "Drive Awhile for Freedom": Brooklyn CORE's 1964 Stall-In and Public Discourse on Protest Violence." In *Groundwork: Local Black Freedom Movements in America,* edited by Jeanne Theoharis and Komozi Woodard. New York: New York University Press, 2005.

———. "Revolution Has Come to Brooklyn: Construction Trades Protests and the Negro Revolt of 1963." In *Black Power at Work: Community Control, Affirmative Action, and the Construction Industry,* edited by David Goldberg and Trevor Griffey. Ithaca, NY: ILR Press, 2010.

Richardson, James. *Willie Brown: A Biography.* Berkeley: University of California Press, 1996.

Sutton, Percy. "In Nomination for the Presidency, the Name of Shirley Chisholm." *Massachusetts Review* 13, no. 4 (1972): 707.

Theoharis, Jeanne. *The Rebellious Life of Mrs. Rosa Parks.* Boston: Beacon Press, 2013.

Tree, Ronald. *A History of Barbados.* London: Granada, 1972.

Wilder, Craig Steven. *A Covenant with Color: Race and Social Power in Brooklyn.* New York: Columbia University Press, 2000.

Worrell, Rodney. *Pan-Africanism in Barbados: An Analysis of the Activities of the Major 20th-Century Pan-African Formation in Barbados.* Published by Rodney Worrell, 2002.

INDEX